THE PILLARS OF GYNARCHY

The Pillars of Gynarchy

VIOLA VOLTAIRINE

Artvamp Books

CONTENTS

PART 3
GYNARCHY-ALIGNED EDUCATION

FEMDOM AS RELIGION

PART 4
THE DEVI DOCTRINE

PART 5
SHADOW AND VIRUS

Artvamp Books is a division of:
Artvamp, LLC
6525 Gunpark Drive
Suite 370, Box 106
Boulder, Colorado 80301
artvamp.com

ISBN 979-8-9890097-0-1 (paperback)
ISBN 979-8-9890097-6-3 (eBook)

First printed 2023

A NEW PARADIGM

"Look for the truth that explodes existing boundaries and definitions. Follow your instincts and you'll get a chance to break prevailing rules so beautifully you may even end up establishing a new norm, a new paradigm. Nothing frozen is perfect."

Nadya Tolokonnikova
Read & Riot: A Pussy Riot Guide to Activism

FOREWORD AND ACKNOWLEDGEMENTS

As I finish this book's final edits, I have a pack of proof-readers, mostly male, combing over it, correcting typos and grammar, checking facts, and offering up their thoughts, feelings, and opinions. As a result, they are also sending me books, videos, and articles that are directly related to the topics within. I am enjoying being surprised by the endless connections, like one article on how the Vatican was built on a necropolis - an ancient cemetery - named after the Etruscan Goddess, Vatika, Queen of the Underworld, and that her name is related to the Latin word for vagina. It gave me a giggle to know that, not only am I correct about Christian orthodoxy deliberately trying to trample and squash a long history of Devi worship, but that, just as I have a tendency to assert in random Twitter rants, they really *are* a death cult. And you know, obvious jokes about the papal pussy palace are also fun.

Sacrilegious jabs aside, one recent article in particular raised a point that needs to be highlighted in any discussion of Gynarchy. Though gender roles are changing, and we understand that gender is more of a spectrum than strictly defined boxes, most people don't want to live in an androgynous world. If you do, that's fine, but most of us who engage in some form of heterosexual romance still kinda like gender differences. We know, both intuitively and backed up by research, that there are legitimate social, biological, behavioral, and even a few neurological differences between men and women, and we rather enjoy them. As Washington Post columnist, Christine Emba put it:

> *"Biology isn't destiny — there is no one script for how to be a woman or a man. But despite a push by some advocates to make everything from bathrooms to birthing gender-neutral, most people don't actually want a completely androgynous society. And if a new model for masculinity is going to find popular appeal, it will depend on putting the distinctiveness of men to good use in whatever form it comes."*

As women begin to rise in terms of education and independence, and concepts of gender itself are getting an overhaul, men are left with outmoded roles of masculinity that just don't fit them and end up feeling lost about what it means to be a "real" man. Misogynistic models like Andrew Tate and well-meaning but regressive professors like Jordan Peterson have stepped up to fill the vacuum. But they're only doubling down on the stale and often anti-feminine narratives, making matters even worse. They create further schisms. Straight women seem to be just one more misogynistic comment away from joining the 4B movement – a lifestyle started in South Korea of women refusing heterosexual marriage (bihon), childbearing (bichulsan), dating (biyeonae), and sex with men (bisekseu). Meanwhile, men, on average, are more depressed and lonelier than ever.

> *"Past models of masculinity feel unreachable or socially unacceptable; new ones have yet to crystallize. What are men for in the modern world? What do they look like? Where do they fit? These are social questions but also ones with major political ramifications. Whatever self-definition men settle on will have an enormous impact on society."* (Emba)

To discover those updated definitions of a man, we must know how to embrace distinctive qualities of masculinity and put them to good use. Masculine traits like strength, risk-taking, systemizing, protecting, providing, and problem-solving are all positive attributes, so long as they are not perverted by ego and male anxiety over hierarchy or humiliation, and so long as they don't get conflated with men repressing their emotions or oppressing women.

I often get comments on my podcasts like "She's a man-hater." My students and devotees know that this could not be further from the truth. I have learned from them about the pain men have been through as they grapple with who they are and their place in society. And when I unfold the higher nature of the Feminine and the masculine for them, spelling out how their common attributes can be supportive of life rather than destructive or toxic, they find peace. What a relief to know how to be the best version of a man you can be! What a relief to be accepted and cherished!

These are my evolved men. They don't need to prove anything to anyone. Their manhood is not on trial. They don't feel their sense of self is ripped away because women have power or set firm boundaries. They are good men. The men of the future.

Contrary to popular sentiment, most women don't want to be rid of men. We're just tired of the kind of masculinity that feels like a boot on our necks, a roofie in our drinks, and piss on the toilet seat. So, even as I push back hard against the atrocities of the patriarchy and the devaluation of the Feminine by a male-dominated society, I look at these evolved men as the remedy, not the malady. Their impact on the world is enormous, and they should be recognized for that.

...

In recognition, I would like to thank my two live-in subs, Drum and Robbi, who fed me, did my laundry and dishes, helped with childcare, listened to my ramblings about religion and philosophy, rubbed my feet, drove me to the hospital, and nursed me through hernia surgery, loved me, watched movies and read books with me, and proofread the earliest drafts. My pet and my domestic sissy - you are the seeds of the Hive that started it all.

I want to thank my beloved dasa, Brett, who has been instrumental in keeping my courses running smoothly, organizing my online life, supporting trainees, and setting up the infrastructure for my international organization of Dominant

Women called The Company. You were truly the first man to fully grasp my ideology and put it into action in a very real way. I also want to thank your wife Suzanne for graciously loaning you out to me to fulfill the Desires of Devi.

I also want to thank my most dedicated devotees and trainees who have asked the right kinds of questions to help clarify my writing and poured over a chapter at a time to catch my missed commas and awkward sentences. To the evolved men: Wayne, CJ, Max (demon), Marti, Goodrock, jiva, Christopher, Win, Maidy, Buster, and all my darlings on the Cathexis House community Discord server. Your support has been crucial. You have been such good boys!

For inspiration, open communication, and showing me what sisterhood looks like, I want to thank the Oracles and the Mistresses of The Company. You jumped right in to play and made the experiment a success. I love to watch us all grow and flourish, genuinely taking pleasure in our dominance. I also want to thank Kasia Urbaniak for being the central node in the network, and for giving us a language of power that expresses all the things we needed to uncover and unearth to become unbound. A round of applause for all our bad girls, and for love!

Big thanks to Sylvie and Vixx, and MaitresseX for help with the FemDom research! Sylvie, you've been a strong support from the beginning of Cathexis House, and the connections and discoveries have been enriching.

I also owe a little gratitude to my non-submissive but always gracious Twitter friend Jack, who kept me honest and accurate and challenged the blind spots in my thinking in ways that helped refine and polish this book. You prove online discourse between people with differing viewpoints doesn't have to go off the rails.

And finally, thanks to my offspring, for fiercely standing up for their identity and for the whole LGBTQIA+ community, and for playing this song on repeat so many times that it got stuck in my head:

I wear women's underwear
And then I go to strike a pose in my full-length mirror
I cross my legs just like a queer
But my libido is strong when a lady is near, ya
What defines a straight man's straight?
Is it the boxer in the briefs or a 12-ounce steak? Nah!
     Verbatim, by Mother Mother

I love you all.

Goddess Viola Strepsata Voltairine
(Ms. V if you're nasty)
New Moon, August 16, 2023

Surrender, Submit, Sacrifice, Serve, Survive
To Her, For Her, Through Her

PART 1

THE REASONS

Spring appears when the time is right
Women are violets coming to light
Don't underestimate the making of life
The planet has a funny way of stopping a fight
Mother Nature's dying
Nobody's keeping score
I don't wanna live in a man's world anymore
                    Marina, *Man's World*

| 1 - 1 |

The Stories We Tell

In 2020 artists Judy Chicago and Nadya Tolokonnikova collaborated on a participatory project asking What if Women Ruled the World? Hand-sewn banners presented questions like "Would There Be Violence?" "Would The Earth Be Protected?" "Would There Be Private Property?" "Would God be Female?"

From the website https://dminti.com/whatifwomen-ruledtheworld/: *"This project took Chicago's inspiring banners 'What If Women Ruled the World', which were created in collaboration with Maria Grazia Chiuri for the Dior Spring Summer 2020 Haute Couture show, as its source for a new revolutionary blockchain enabled call-and-response."*

Our lives and our world are shaped by the questions we ask, and even more so by the stories we tell ourselves and each other in answer to those questions. More intensely in the past five years, I have noticed both women and men collectively pondering the question "What if women ruled the world?" and coming up with a variety of stories of what it might look like. In my first book, *150 Years of Gynarchy,* Natalia Stroika presented a vision of a world of female supremacy, where cooperation, collaboration, community, and women's health were centered. The picture she painted was quite comforting.

As we have progressed, the collective buzz is taking a different shape. It is quietly changing from asking "if we ruled" to "when we rule." We are imagining how it will come about, with fewer doubts that it is already gestating as some certain and not-too-distant female-led future.

So what stories are we telling about the potential of a woman-led world? And how might those stories transpire?

To begin, I turned to A.I. for answers, asking ChatGPT to write an essay on the potential advantages of Matriarchy. Surprisingly, I was not at all disappointed in the result. It didn't waffle, reassuring the reader that it was just presenting one opinion and might be wrong, as I have noted ChatGPT tends to do with controversial topics. Without any specific prompting, it gave me a simple list of advantages, and all, serendipitously, are points that were already contained in the outline of this very book. Here is the essay in full, which took A.I. all of two minutes to write:

Title: The Potential Advantages of Matriarchy: A Paradigm Shift Towards Equality and Balance

Introduction: Matriarchy, as a social system where women

hold primary power and leadership roles, stands in contrast to the historically prevalent patriarchy. While patriarchy has long dominated societies, it is worth exploring the potential advantages of matriarchy as a means to foster equality, balance, and social well-being. This essay aims to investigate the potential benefits of matriarchy, shedding light on the positive consequences it could bring to various aspects of society.

1. *Gender Equality: One of the significant advantages of matriarchy lies in its potential to address the persistent gender inequalities present in patriarchal societies. Matriarchal systems strive to empower women by placing them in positions of leadership, decision-making, and influence. By breaking traditional gender roles and challenging gender stereotypes, matriarchy can contribute to a more inclusive society that values and respects the inherent worth and capabilities of all individuals, regardless of their gender.*

2. *Nurturing and Compassionate Leadership: Matriarchal societies often emphasize nurturing and compassionate leadership styles. Historically, women have been associated with qualities such as empathy, cooperation, and consensus-building. By placing women in positions of power, matriarchy can promote leadership traits that prioritize collaboration, emotional intelligence, and social cohesion. Such leadership approaches have the potential to foster more inclusive and holistic decision-making processes that take into*

account a broader range of perspectives and contribute to the well-being of the community as a whole.

3. *Environmental Stewardship: Many studies have suggested a positive correlation between women's empowerment and environmental sustainability. Matriarchy emphasizes the idea of nurturing and preserving life, which aligns with the sustainable management of natural resources. Women, as primary caregivers and often intimately connected to their environments, tend to exhibit a greater concern for environmental sustainability. By empowering women in decision-making roles, matriarchy can potentially lead to more environmentally conscious policies, resource management practices, and a renewed focus on preserving our planet for future generations.*

4. *Reduction in Violence and Conflict: Patriarchy has often perpetuated systems of violence, domination, and aggression. In contrast, matriarchal societies, with their emphasis on nurturing and collaboration, have the potential to reduce violence and conflict. By prioritizing peaceful resolutions, promoting dialogue, and valuing the interconnectedness of all individuals, matriarchy can foster a culture of non-violence and empathy. This shift may lead to a decrease in interpersonal violence, armed conflicts, and the marginalization of certain groups, ultimately creating safer and more harmonious communities.*

5. *Holistic Approach to Health and Well-being: Matriarchal societies tend to prioritize holistic approaches to health and*

well-being. The emphasis on nurturing, care, and community support can contribute to the development of comprehensive healthcare systems that address the physical, emotional, and mental needs of individuals. By valuing the well-being of all community members, matriarchy has the potential to reduce health disparities and promote overall societal well-being.

Conclusion: While matriarchy is not a panacea for all societal challenges, exploring its potential advantages opens up opportunities for reimagining gender roles, leadership styles, and social structures. By promoting gender equality, nurturing leadership, environmental stewardship, reducing violence, and prioritizing holistic well-being, matriarchy offers a vision of a more balanced and equitable society.

About half of the men I talk to online agree that these advantages are a likely outcome of women's leadership. And they aren't alone. In his 2011 book *The Better Angels of Our Nature*, Steven Pinker points out that the 20th century, though still quite horrific, was the least violent century we have on record. And the reason for this, he suggests, could be boiled down to two factors: democracy and "feminization." Because of the slow and still incomplete empowerment of women, and the rise of feminine values, everyone's lives became safer.

The other half (and a few pessimistic women) cling to the myth that women in power will act precisely the same as men in power and things would be just as bad with women in control. "Power tends to corrupt, and absolute power corrupts absolutely," they quote Lord Acton, an English Catholic historian, politician, and writer who died in 1902. Acton was gone more than two decades before Nikola Tesla declared that women would rule the world by 2026, our intellect far surpassing men's after having been held back for so long, and that we would run things more like the society of the venerable honeybee. In Tesla's vision:

> *"This struggle of the human female toward sex equality will end in a new sex order, with the female as superior. The modern woman, who anticipates in merely superficial phenomena the advancement of her sex, is but a surface symptom of something deeper and more potent fermenting in the bosom of the race.*

> *It is not in the shallow physical imitation of men that women will assert first their equality and later their superiority, but in the awakening of the intellect of women.*

> *Through countless generations, from the very beginning, the social subservience of women resulted naturally in the partial atrophy or at least the hereditary suspension of mental qualities which we now know the female sex to be endowed with no less than men.*

> *But the female mind has demonstrated a capacity for all the mental acquirements and achievements of men. As generations ensue that capacity will be expanded; the average*

> *woman will be as well educated as the average man, and then better educated, for the dormant faculties of her brain will be stimulated to an activity that will be all the more intense and powerful because of centuries of repose. Woman will ignore precedent and startle civilization with their progress.*
>
> *The acquisition of new fields of endeavor by women, their gradual usurpation of leadership, will dull and finally dissipate feminine sensibilities and human civilisation draw closer and closer to the perfect civilization of the bee."*

Nikola Tesla was confident the power of women could only advance society, not simply mimic the ideas nor the mistakes of men.

However, New York Times Best Selling author Naomi Alderman seems to be one of those pessimists who think that if women suddenly gained unequal power, they would inevitably engage in violence and coercion to harm and oppress men. In her book *The Power* teenage girls begin discovering that they can shoot bolts of electricity from their bodies thanks to the awakening of a new (or possibly long dormant) organ across their collarbone called a skein. Most young women develop this power around age 15 and can awaken it in older women as well. I do recommend the book. I began reading it with great enthusiasm, having seen the first season of its adaptation as a TV series beforehand. The idea of women living in a world finally safe from the threat of ubiquitous male violence is refreshing and hopeful. I want to see more.

Disappointingly, toward the end of the book, Alderman gave up on the idea of a better world run by women. She fell back on the tired old adage of old Catholic Lord Acton and could not seem to bring herself to fully envision anything outside of patriarchal styles and patterns of power. She didn't imagine that power could be wielded differently. It feels like she threw up her hands and gave in to the dominant rhetoric. Let's hope that can change with the development of the second season of the TV series (if there is a second season). The show deviates from the book in significant ways, and I'm hoping she has the opportunity to rethink the imagined future that she has the power to write. I hope through this process she learns to trust and believe in her fellow women as a class.

Power does not always corrupt. That's nothing more than a believable but tired old myth. As presidential biographer Robert Caro states, *"Power doesn't corrupt, it reveals."* It reveals the nature and character of those holding it. Caro says, *"Power can cleanse. What I believe is always true about power is that power always reveals. When you have enough power to do what you always wanted to do, then you see what the guy always wanted to do."*

Let's take just a moment to define power succinctly. Power is simply the unhampered ability to do what you want, as Caro points out. And as I will present later, there is a mound of evidence that women wield power in much different ways than men and want to run things in ways in which men don't seem capable of running them. The evidence points to women concerning themselves with the betterment of the group (family, community, country) as a whole, not just the enrichment of themselves. As Nikola Tesla might point out, the Queen cannot survive without a thriving hive. It appears, however, that too many people would prefer to ignore that evidence in order to save men's feelings. In this time and culture, we sure do quite a lot of back-bending in order to allow men to save face and not be blamed or shamed individually for their abysmal track record as a group. I think it's time we stop pandering.

Another dystopian vision of a woman-led world is found in the book *The Quickening* by Talulah Riley. In the book all of the world's tensions come to a head and charismatic revolutionary Dana Mayer has a manifesto in place, called *The Quickening*, named after the feeling women have when they realize they are pregnant. "The world is pregnant," she declares, and she is ready to take advantage of the moment to birth a whole new direction for her country. One where women lead and cooperation, order, and aesthetics are guiding principles. She's a shrewd visionary sociopath but dedicated to making the world a better place. It's a vision of Matriarchy as a comfortable, peaceful, pleasing kind of fascism. Women are safe, but men, as you might have guessed, have their freedoms completely curtailed.

In the book, straight men are allowed only three options. 1.) become workers isolated in separate men's encampments and be employed to tear down remnants of the old world, including any buildings that are ugly or phallic; 2.) become gentlemen who are lady's pets in gilded cages; or 3.) become eunuchs - the Non-Gendered People who have more freedoms than both of the other categories.

This dystopia is also anti-Internet. The pace of life is slowed. But even men note that things run surprisingly efficiently and smoothly, much more so than before "The Change." Women are not supposed to work while on their periods, and instead freebleed in luxurious bath houses. The middle and upper-class women don't bother with pregnancy. Child rearing is farmed out to seaside resorts called Children's Towns where young fertile "Sisters" are used as baby factories (though it is mentioned that the technology for artificial wombs is being developed to relieve them of this burdensome duty). Children intermingle until age twelve when the boys' fates are chosen for them. Many are simply sold off to fight in foreign wars. Personal autonomy seems to be reserved, as it always has been in reality, to the ruling class.

As you can guess, the fascist utopia is not a happy place for many men. Even the beloved gentlemen are bound to highly restrictive codes of language and behavior befitting their class and social status. They are overseen by armed female guards. And this whole concept follows the other sadly misguided assumption that people often make that, in order for women to rule, men will have to be oppressed with a heavy hand, and that some grand hierarchical state apparatus backed by violence must be held in place to maintain order. How sadly pessimistically patriarchal, once again. *The Quickening* reads like a cross between carefully created anti-gynarchy propaganda warning against the inevitable horror of allowing women to take over, and a super hot sadistic femdom fantasy. It practically begs men to stop the inevitable shift of power or accept oppression, humiliation, and sometimes outright torture.

Of course, some kinksters and female supremacists among my circles are incredibly turned on by this notion of a strictly controlled matriarchal fascist utopia. There are men who would love to be overpowered and squashed under the heel of the opposite sex. There are women who are done with playing nice and want to bring men to heel. This is understandable. And it's always sexy when done with consent and care. But unfortunately, I don't see it as sustainable, nor is it conducive to the peace and well-being of our communities as a whole. Force is always met with counterforce and backlash. We've been playing that game much too long as human beings and we need to change tactics. It's time to rewrite the script and get rid of the old time-worn clichés. We need to be smarter about all of this. Smarter, more thoughtful, and broader-minded than patriarchy.

Although both Alderman and Riley espouse two different versions of the same disappointing "power corrupts" fallacy, it is interesting to note that both books came out within a year of one another and demonstrate a theme currently vibrating through the collective consciousness. That theme is the end of male domination. Until now, aside from femdom erotica, not much fiction has been written that imagines a world where women overturn patriarchy to such an extent that they can feel totally safe and in complete control of their lives. Most fiction involving matriarchy fits into the category of that endless supply of schlocky cheap romance where women from strong female-led communities encounter the opposite sex and suddenly become fawning and submissive, overcome by their intoxicating attraction to manly men! I am sure you can sense my eye roll here, without even having to see me.

Both *The Quickening* and *The Power* are books dear to my heart, they are exceptionally well-written, exciting, courageous, and I highly recommend them. There are parts of each of them that are so inspiring and bring me such joy that I want to cry and hug the authors in thanks. I am only so biting in my criticism because I am hungry for a more serious literary exploration around how women rule differently, and it proves difficult to find.

It seems some women authors are thoroughly enjoying the fantasies of unlimited power, but they are still too timid to buy into it as a reality. Perhaps they are still a bit brainwashed into believing what the contemporary patriarchy would have us believe: That men and women behave the same, want the same things, and that only equality is fair (as I will show, it is far from true fairness); That all we really need is a bigger slice of the patriarchy pie for ourselves and we'll be free (spoiler: we won't). Perhaps Gynarchy seems like a fairytale to them, something far away, unreachable, an abstraction. Perhaps they are afraid that if they really embrace the idea that women could do better, they may be disappointed. Or perhaps I am being a bit too harsh, in that the primary intent behind their books was not to paint the picture of a possible world, as inspiring as it is to see women safe and free and powerful, but to act as criticisms of patriarchy, shining a bright light on how men have behaved by casting them as women and presenting the whole scenario in reverse.

These new rumblings around the end of male domination are not just in fiction, however. Women's groups are cropping up everywhere and in women's only back channels across the internet and in small circles of friends, we discuss what we really want and how we will inevitably get it. We talk about power and how to use it. We talk about how to support and uplift one another instead of competing with one another. And there's something left out of the above books that I will discuss in later chapters: we talk about women as the embodiment of love.

Speaking of love stories, I found one fictional narrative at least a bit more plausible in terms of what might happen when women rule the world. It is in the movie *No Men Beyond This Point*, a 2015 mockumentary written and directed by Mark Sawers. Conveniently though, the movie takes the most troublesome aspect of the transition to a woman-led world out of the equation. That aspect being men. Men are going extinct. The story goes that in 1952 women began reproducing through parthenogenesis - spontaneous fertilization without the need for sex. All of their babies are female. Slowly fewer and fewer women can reproduce through intercourse. It's as if nature decided men were no longer necessary, and just phased them out over the course of 60 or so years. As I discuss in a future chapter, this is not an impossible scenario. There is some evidence that the Y chromosome is going extinct, though it will take millions of years for that to happen, not just a few decades.

In *No Men Beyond This Point*, there are some men left, however. And a movement of separatism begins wherein the men are sent off to extremely comfortable camps where they don't need to work and are completely taken care of with delicious healthy buffets and plenty of entertainment to live out the rest of their lives peacefully as the last remaining men on earth. There's a men's movement, but it doesn't gain much momentum as the well-fed and cared for men are relatively content with their lot.

In this vision, women can do every job men can do, and do them better. This includes diplomacy. There is no more war because the women of the world get into sync (literally, even their menstrual periods sync up) and can agree on collective goals for the planet. The human race thrives like never before.

Women still pair up to raise children but don't always have romantic feelings for, or sexual attraction to, each other. Some men stay in society working as domestic help, and the mockumentary focuses on Andrew, the youngest man alive at age 35. He is the housekeeper and babysitter for a female pair and their daughters. The two women's relationship is nothing more than that of close friends and is not all that intimate. And it happens that Andrew and one of his employers, Iris, fall in love.

Because science has advanced in this society to a point where most biological diseases, problems, and ailments can be cured (yay for women taking control of medicine!), small handfuls of scientists are looking into the possibility of facilitating sexual reproduction once again. Many women are against working to reintroduce sexual fertilization, seeing the evolution to parthenogenesis as part of nature's sacred plan (Punctuating their arguments with the exclamation, "Praise nature!"). Others realize they actually kind of like having men around and that they should not be allowed to go extinct entirely. Eventually the story breaks of Andrew and his employer's love affair, and it's decided to try to help them get pregnant the old-fashioned way. Men may not die out after all, since the consensus of women is that they should be given another chance.

There are a few things I like about this scenario. The remaining men are not oppressed. They are treated with care and dignity, subdued through nurturing, despite the protests of a handful of activists who don't want to see their gender go extinct. Of course, the small number of men left, and the premise that they are going extinct, solves the problem of men struggling against female power. There is no real opposition left. Women are free to rule as they want. Secondly, I like that this vision illustrates what I feel to be an accurate outcome of women running the world. A sense of cooperation and a collective striving for the health and well-being of the entire planet becomes the norm. An almost psychic link and intimate understanding between all women worldwide is accomplished. The hive mentality Nikola Tesla imagined is realized. And finally, I like that the women ultimately decide that letting the men die out completely is not fair and act to do something about it. Because they are loving and caring human beings who want the best outcomes for everyone. And some women really love men. This speaks to the notion that women are themselves the embodiment of love.

And here's where people argue that women would still fight among themselves and vie for power over one another. But as I said, the evidence of the opposite, especially when women are not forced to claw their way into power within brutal, competitive, patriarchal, hierarchical structures, is very strong. In an argument between women behaving like men and women creating whole new ways of dealing with power, as I will demonstrate, my side of the debate simply has more supporting data. All the opposing side has is a handful of examples of patriarchal females like Margaret Thatcher. Women behaving like men to gain a foothold in a world run by men is *not* evidence of how Gynarchy will play out. On the contrary, it's only another example of how patriarchy works to negate the feminine.

Of course, getting men out of the equation to pave the way for Gynarchy is not at all feasible, nor is it even desirable to most of us. Despite having been harmed by them over and over, most women still love men (at least some of them). So the transition to power will not be as smooth as in *No Men Beyond This Point*. It is messier and cannot happen en masse worldwide all at once. And it can NOT happen through violent revolution or force like in *The Quickening* or *The Power*. Research is clear that violent overthrows never lead to lasting power change. They only breed resentment and foment unrest in the long term. We must use our brains and hearts, not violence and brawn to move into this new era. Men make war. Women make connections. Men compete for dominance. Women birth whole societies. As Dana says in *The Quickening*, we must create this "in the shape of a woman."

Which brings me to the purpose of this book. It is meant to be both a philosophical and practical guide. The Pillars of Gynarchy are a moral code and a step-by-step process for planting the seeds of change that will grow wild and alter the course of your world. If you already know you want to live in a woman-led community, let this book be your blueprint. Use it. Play with it, riff off of it. Build upon it in your own way. And reach out to me to let me know what works for you. Let's build networks and learn from one another.

If, on the other hand, you've made up your mind that Gynarchy is not for you, and if you are convinced that women running things is a stupid idea, unfair, impossible, or a nightmare, then this book is just not for you. I am not here to convince you to live in a world you don't want to live in. Here in the U.S. and all over the world, there are patriarchies in which to situate yourself very comfortably, and you need never even give it a second thought. You are still the majority, so rest easy. Stay firmly where you are, and chances are you'll still be able to enjoy male dominance throughout this lifetime. Plural ideologies are possible, and to stray from the mainstream requires an active choice ("with open eyes and an open heart"). No need to argue or upset yourself over my ideas. They probably won't affect your life at all. We'll do our thing, and you do yours. There is no need to bark, huff and puff, or write angry tweets and emails. Don't act so frightened. No one wants to harm you. You are safe.

We become the stories we tell about ourselves. Take care in writing yours. Attune it to your authentic values, desires, hopes, and philosophy of living. And don't let anyone else's plans deter you. As for both the established and budding

Gynarchists: Come along with me. Join me in envisioning not *if*, but *how* this movement now unfolds. Let's see what happens when we women rule our worlds.

| 1-2 |

Gynarchy Defined

In my book *150 Years of Gynarchy,* I refer to Gynarchy as "a parallel existence with its own rules. An underground religion with its own rites and moral guidelines - one that combines the kinky sexuality of FemDom with the social and political fire of feminism and the spiritual zeal of Goddess worship and witchcraft." It is, in fact, a way of life guided by the overarching principle that women are powerful, and important, and deserve to be protected from harm, to be supported, and to have their authentic desires realized. The bold claim I make here is that women are natural leaders and rulers, and men can find unmatched fulfillment in support-ing, serving, and pleasing us, allowing us to guide and direct them. Many men crave that role, no matter how they disguise it or deny it. Women have been used to hold up the world while men strive and compete continuously to try to prove that they have worth. Their ways are currently based on ego and insecurity. The concerted efforts of patriarchal religion to reverse nature and place women under men as helpmates, objects, and baby factories so they can go about conquering things and feeding their egos is perverse, unnatural, and is causing great destruction to our planet. If it isn't readily apparent to you just by opening your eyes and taking a look around, I have evidence to back up this claim which I will outline in future chapters.

The word Gynarchy has been used in many different contexts, so it's helpful first to go back to the original definition of the word. As far as I can tell, it first came about in the 1970s. *The Dictionary of Feminist Theory* has an entry for "Gynarchism." It reads:

> *"Feminist anarchists believe that if a 'gynarchy' created by women replaced patriarchy it would not replicate the same forms of hierarchy. The term is sometimes elided with 'matriarchy', and Charlotte Perkins Gilman used one version of the term - 'gynaeocracy.'"*

It began as a political proposition. As I reclaim the word from the entanglements of pornography, I return it to its roots. Gyn - Women, and Anarchy - the organization of society on the basis of voluntary cooperation, without political institutions or hierarchical government. Gynarchy is a fully voluntary society where women hold the power and authority. That power is not only about power over others, but when it is, that is a fully consensual arrangement toward certain goals and ends that serve the community as a whole. It's essentially anarchism led by women, where men voluntarily take a back seat when it comes to designing and running things. They do so because they believe in the natural authority of women, because they desire being ruled by women, and because they think it is the best way forward. Their motives are not to gain access to sex or advancement for themselves alone, but to support the women so that the community thrives.

Many people don't understand what anarchism is. Set aside your assumptions, as they won't be useful to your understanding. Let's keep it simple. Put succinctly, anarchism is a cooperative horizontally organized consensual societal structure. That's it. In terms of Gynarchy, many women work together in equal roles to oversee the smooth functioning of their communities. Like with bees, hives form around individual women. Men, and sometimes even other women, who respect a specific woman leader will gather around her and be guided into roles where their skills and interests best serve her vision. And those many women make up a vast network of equal nodes, communicating, and sharing knowledge and resources to best direct their individual hives and live in harmony with the other hives.

Any hierarchies within the myriad of roles surrounding each woman are purely temporary and functional. The teacher/student hierarchy is one example, wherein the hierarchy dissolves once the student achieves the same aptitude as the teacher. Our "queen bees" are like the power station of each hive. They give each community cohesion, direction, vision, and central purpose. They are the energetic center of the social organism. Everyone moves closer and farther away from her within the circle surrounding her as needed to perform their roles and for the hive to function.

Gynarchy is matrilineal and matrilocal. All power flows from a woman to her female successor, which may be her daughter or someone she has trained to eventually take on a central position. The house or estate of the "queen bee" is where all the action is concentrated and all decisions that affect the group are made. And when hives grow too big to be harmonious and stable, another woman may take on the responsibility of beginning a new hive, splitting off from the original. She then becomes a part of the vast network of queen bees with access to their collective knowledge and resources.

Gynarchy is meant to exist as a collection of smaller communities, held together by common principles and ideology. It is my opinion that nations often become too large to create cohesive, peaceful, smooth-functioning wholes. Large nations become unwieldy and require endless bureaucracy and policing to run. We were not meant to live like that. Small autonomous communities work best. And these will naturally form coalitions with other small autonomous communities.

In the distant future, I can imagine abolishing nations and borders altogether. But as I warn again and again, for now, we must begin as small nodes in a network and live inside of or perhaps superimposed over the current forms of government. This is not a sudden violent revolution where we take over the world in a bluster of pronouncements and swift actions. We don't charge in dicks out, guns ablaze. We aren't as reckless and short-sighted as men. Think of the most common method wicked women use to murder. They do it discreetly, with poison. We will slowly create an alternative that eventually attracts enough people to become more and more viable, our ideas will spread, and gently, methodically, organically - like weaving a magic spell - we'll choke out patriarchy over time. Always remember, we are playing the long game.

Its node-like nature is one reason I refer to Gynarchy as a religion rather than just a political movement. Religions are a powerful glue. Like every religion there will be sects all over the world, each doing things in their own way, and joined together in a common set of beliefs and values. These beliefs and values are what I call the Pillars of Gynarchy. There is no central authority. Just a shared ideology and a shared sense of belonging. There are common rites and common teachings. In terms of spirituality, we may not all center the same Goddess or aspect of the Goddess or The Mother of Creation. But we all refer to the source of our existence as the Feminine.

Gynarchy is a social, political, spiritual, and sexual power. I know some of you can feel the erotic stirrings of your life force just thinking about it. Power, simply defined, is the ability to get what you need and want. Authority is to take the role of the author; now is the time we start writing new rules and principles to live by.

| 1 - 3 |

The Argument Against Egalitarian Society

"Fair is fair!" The Legend of Billie Jean, 1985

What if? What if patriarchy had created a harmonious world? What if when men were in charge, we all had a life of ease and abundance rather than constant survival stress for the majority, while a small percentage lived in luxury? What if under patriarchy there was no war or senseless violence? No horrors of mass destruction or genocide? What if under patriarchy the vulnerable were protected instead of bullied or hunted? What if men had harnessed resources in a way that worked in concert with nature rather than causing environmental damage? What if women were safe and cherished under patriarchy and could walk the streets topless and free without harassment or attack? What if patriarchy really was life-supporting rather than conquering, colonizing and exploitative? Why did it have to go the opposite direction? Why did men fuck it up so badly? And having failed so miserably as a group, why would we ever trust them to have even 50% of the power and authority over our lives?

Do I need to list the wars and bloody battles men have started and sent their fellow men to die in the past 2000 years? There were literally thousands, with several mass genocides (Armenia, Germany, Rwanda) in the 20th century alone. I had a boyfriend who used to refer to the History Channel as "The War Channel" because men who write history tend to mark time by recounting "great" battles and who conquered who. Do I need to list the murders in the name of a father god in the common era? There are tens of thousands. The number of rapes committed by men daily? There is one every 98 seconds in the U.S. alone. More than 570 per day. Even if we consider that between 2% and 10% could be false reports, it would bring that number down to 513, conservatively.

We are all aware of these stats, aren't we? Despite the outcries that "Women rape too," and "Women murder too," there is the glaring and undeniable fact that the majority of all violent crime against both men and women is committed by men. Just a glance at the FBI's website shows the numbers. The only crime that women even come close to competing with men in is embezzlement, and that's still by less than half. If it were a contest, men win at rape at 99.1%, murder at 88.7%, and arson at 82%. When men say they want to be women's protectors, they are not offering to protect us against wolves and bears. They are offering to protect us against other men.

So by what logic should we entrust them with any

percentage of the power over our futures? In what world does that make any sense? In this respect, men and women have never been equal, which is a huge compliment to women.

Many men are not violent, one may protest. Some men make compassionate leaders, one might argue in their defense. Yes, well the exception only highlights the rule, as they say. And one might be appalled that I would lump men like Gandhi, St. Francis of Assisi, or the Buddha in with all the rest, however, these were men who still upheld oppressive male dominance despite their capacity for empathy, which I would argue is only a further indictment of the general nature of men. Yes, even Gautam Buddha himself discriminated against female followers, reinforcing ideas that women were incomplete, their bodies unfit to obtain enlightenment.

And what of the argument that "we just didn't know better?" I'm told by men that, in general, they mean well, and they think they are doing the right thing. They're just clueless regarding the effects their systems and leadership have had on half the population. Last time I checked, cluelessness is not a positive quality to be sought out in a person of authority.

> *"Here's all you have to know about men and women: women are crazy, men are stupid. And the main reason women are crazy is that men are stupid."* George Carlin, comedian

So why now do we suddenly completely redefine the concept of fairness in order to coddle men? Is the reality of their collective harms and failures too bitter a pill for them to swallow? Why do we still have this desire to uphold male privilege, ignore history, and give them all a pass?

Let's talk about fairness. In *150 Years of Gynarchy,* I used the cookie analogy to illustrate true fairness. You have a brother and sister. You give them each a cookie. The brother steals his sister's cookie and eats both cookies. Boys will be boys. So you give them each a second cookie. He does it again. He steals his sister's cookie and eats both. Sister is feeling quite fed up by now. Brother's pretty happy with the whole deal. Do we just keep giving the boy more cookies? Do we take the last cookie in the jar, break it in half, and give half of a cookie to each child? Then finally MAYBE the sister gets half of a cookie, if and only if the brother can learn to behave himself? Or do we finally say, "Son, you've had enough," and excuse him from the table while we give the sister a whole damned cookie? Any child could tell you the ethical answer.

If we want to be fair, investing our hopes in an egalitarian society at this point is a cruel joke. It is the antithesis of fairness. I have brought it up in my last book, but the late great Justice Ruth Bader Ginsburg made a point I wish all of us could absorb and understand.

> *"When I'm sometimes asked when will there be enough [women on the Supreme Court]? And I say when there are nine, people are shocked. But there'd been nine men, and nobody's ever raised a question about that."*

Why, after men have had just about 100% of the power

and authority in society for thousands of years, is conceding only 50% now anything close to real fairness? It is not, by any stretch of reason. Not fair nor equal.

Some men will argue that they built civilization as it is now, and therefore men deserve equal authority over it. To that I say, you built it on the backs of women who birthed and nurtured you and took care of your homes, toiling without payment for their 365 days of labor, kept like domestic servants under the authority of fathers and husbands. Men built it because they actively barred women's participation in its creation (and even so a few women made it through against the odds, contributing to things like physics, mathematics, computers, and wireless technology. Women like Émilie du Châtelet, Ada Lovelace, Hedy Lamarr, and Margaret H. Hamilton to name a few). And with only a few exceptions, the things men have built on their own (or often using slave labor) - factories, congested cities, industrial plastics, the combustion engine, monoculture farming, and factory farms - were horrible for the health and wellbeing of humankind. They brought on disease, isolation, depression, and are leading us to environmental catastrophe. After all that, why should we think men are competent at all in designing a viable future? If anything, men have made a giant mess that we are all now left to clean up.

Now here's where men will call on the argument of individualism to try to save their asses. "I personally did nothing wrong. Why do I deserve to give up more than 50% of my authority?"

My answer to this is first that they definitely benefit in sometimes unrecognized and unseen ways from the history and culture of male dominance. You don't have to have it easy to have certain unearned privileges, and some men (black men in the US, immigrants, disabled men, queer men) have fewer than other men. But by and large, being male has more advantages in this world than being female. Not the least of which is a greater sense of safety and autonomy and being taken as more of an authority in comparison to their female counterparts. Are there disadvantages to being male? Sure. And most of those are built into patriarchy itself. Most unfair expectations put on men were designed by other men in the past. Men try to blame women, but the culture of men was not put in place by us. We didn't have the power to set up those roles and standards even if we wanted to.

Men's biggest complaints are 1.) That women have an advantage in custody battles. That is no longer true. In the past 20 years, those laws have changed to give equal power to fathers. But even when it was true, it was only because society expected that women do all of the labor of childrearing, so of course the kids stayed with their moms to spare the men of that burden.

2.) That men have had to fight in wars when women were spared. And to that, I ask which gender waged those wars? That was something men could control, and they decided to march mightily into battle. They could have refused en masse and there would be no war. We'd be forced to find other solutions to conflicts. But it's man's nature to obey authority and follow orders, and the power-hungry ones only know how to use violence to get what they want. War was never an idea women were keen on. Do you really think that we wanted our sons and husbands slaughtered? As early as 411

BCE Aristophanes wrote *Lysistrata*, a play about a woman on a mission to end the Peloponnesian War by denying all the men of the land sex. Historically speaking, though there have been legendary women warriors, it is more typical for women to be anti-war than not. But now women who want to play patriarchal games are allowed into combat positions just like men, so it's a moot point. And if you think the draft, which was only applied to men, was unfair, don't instate a damned draft in the first place. Not for men nor for women. No draft is fair. No war is fair.

And finally, 3.) Men have a higher suicide rate. This is only partially true. Men have a higher success rate at suicide, though women attempt it in higher numbers. And when men cut their lives short, they selfishly leave behind grieving children and spouses who need them, or every once in a while, they take the whole family with them. Men in the United States committed 670 murder-suicides in 2022 alone.

Women would like to take men's depression seriously if only they themselves could bring themselves to talk about it and get help. And I don't mean turning their partners into mothers and therapists all rolled into one. I mean get help from compassionate and skilled professionals who can teach them skills to help excavate, regulate, and resolve any issues they are experiencing. Men's culture discourages proactively dealing with emotions and prefers to repress them until it's impossible to cope. It is getting better, but only marginally so. And this move to change is mostly at the prompting - the pleading - of women.

But I have much more complex reasons why the

individualist "I didn't do it," cop-out is bunk regarding the gendered balance of power. In short, it's about responsibility, epigenetics, and ancestral wounding.

Men would love to pretend that this is year zero and that history can be forgotten, that we can put it behind us, and bury the hatchet. They want us to start fresh as if we've always been equals. But our bodies carry memories from many generations before us and it has an incredible impact on our health and well-being in ways that science is only beginning to understand.

We're not just talking about the anxieties, traumas, and mental afflictions handed down to us through the actions of parents and grandparents due to their own life experiences messing them up psychologically. That's very real, but that's just scratching the surface. We are now starting to understand how our traumas get remembered by the body and how each experience has the capacity to change how our genes work. Chemical markers in our genes react to our environment and to stress hormones. Then those markers get passed down generation after generation. Our bodies remember the suffering and stresses that our great-great-grandparents endured. And it can cause inexplicable diseases and ailments.

Ostensibly, a sudden appearance of ovarian or cervical cancer, when it has never run in your family and you live a healthy lifestyle, might just occur because one of your ancestors was brutally raped and forced to carry her attacker's baby. Perhaps it's not so directly correlated, but it's not improbable. And most certainly, autoimmune disorders and chronic pain, two things that are overwhelmingly more common among women, have provable connections to our epigenome. Our contemporary bodies, and it seems especially women's bodies, hold a record of the stresses of past oppression and inequality.

I find it bizarre that our contemporary Western culture is one of the only cultures that tries to sever our relationships with our ancestors. We are a culture of forgetting. In our misguided quest to be individuals and nothing but individuals, we ignorantly shirk all of our responsibility to be the healers of ancestral wounds. And we bypass a great opportunity to release our future generations from those duties. We pass these wounds and misdeeds down like a hot potato to our kids and their kids until the ancestral load is so heavy it breaks their metaphorical backs, and they'll never know why their backs are broken. Because we also teach them nothing about how to relieve the burden. It's selfish and cruel.

What is ancestral wounding about, and why can it be so harmful to bypass it? If you have frustrating patterns that you have a lot of trouble breaking, especially in relationships, that is likely from ancestral wounding. An ancestral wound will be repeated again and again for generations until it is fully recognized and resolved. If you experience unexplained anxiety or panic attacks, insomnia, dissociation, intrusive thoughts, nightmares, or night terrors, it may not be a personal psychological issue but an unresolved ancestral wound.

In terms of gender relations, you may have a heavy load of regret and guilt built up from how your male ancestors treated women. And you may also have a heavy weight of trauma, fear, and pain that went unresolved among your female ancestors because of how they were treated. You may not feel it in a direct way as regret or trauma, but if you don't address it, it can still affect you. Americans are fools to think we can outrun the ghosts and shadows of the past. They will catch up to us eventually.

In cutting ourselves off from the past we also sever our access to an endless font of wisdom that can be sourced from gaining an understanding of our lineage and finding a psychological link to those who came before us.

> *"Ancestor work is complex and can give us opportunity to reckon with the echoes of how individual family patterns resonate with the current of wider historical conflicts. All of these and more are alive within each of us."* (Quinn - Inlak'ech)

No man is an island. Bringing that truism to work in the context of ancestral healing we can also look to some important thinkers on the matter of our collective memory. Jung wrote about the collective unconscious, wherein the human race stores our common symbols, themes, meanings, dreams, and nightmares that have cropped up across the expanse of our existence again and again. We all have access to this vast database of the collective psyche, and it bubbles up from below our conscious thoughts. Biologist Rupert Sheldrake talks enthusiastically about morphic resonance and morphic fields which hold all memories of everything through all time and create patterns and habits in us and in all living things. History matters. It lives inside us, in our minds, and in our DNA. It created the very foundations of the social structures all around us. There's no real way to escape it.

Setting aside genders that are not part of the classical binary for a moment (I will address those in detail in another chapter), throughout the contiguity of history men belong to a collective class called men, and women belong to a collective class called women. We can protest it all we want, but we all live in context. We exist inside the context of gender and history, and we don't get a say in that. How we deal with it now reverberates well into the future. Keep in mind that we will eventually become ancestors ourselves.

Right now when I hear talk of equality, all I can sense is that women are being thrown a few crumbs and are still not viewed worthy of men's serious respect and consideration on a societal scale. We talk only of equal pay for equal work and getting a bigger piece of the patriarchal pie. If we behave like men inside the structures and hierarchical systems designed by men, then we might be rewarded. A good patriarchal woman can earn more than women have ever earned in the past, but only if she works just a bit harder than a man to prove herself.

Meanwhile, our bodily autonomy is up for debate. In some places, we are still wards of the state, if not of our male partners. We're told we are not to be trusted to make medical decisions for ourselves. Meanwhile, men still think they have a right to our domestic labor and our bodies, and often have no problem forcing the issue if we don't comply, through violence, manipulation, and threats on one hand, and passive-aggressive weaponized incompetence on the other.

There's a lot of lip service to equality - the idea that women can do whatever they want now. We've made progress. We can have bank accounts, own property, and vote. But aside from that it's the same old bullshit. Feminism has not succeeded in gaining our safety or complete agency over our lives. And that's just in America. In places like Iran, Saudi Arabia, and Afghanistan, women struggle to have any personal freedom, and their choices are so restricted as to be utterly suffocating. Whole towns in Eastern Europe subsist on the lucrative market of kidnapping and using women as living fuck dolls for men. Over six million women are forcibly trafficked for sex each year, and tens of thousands of these are here in the U.S. Still more are sold into slavery for domestic and other unpaid labor. We're told how we Western women should stop complaining because we are so lucky and we have it so good. Only in comparison to the absolute hell our sisters elsewhere endure. How low do we set the bar?

An egalitarian society is not even possible as it always defaults to catering to men and their sense of importance. And even as they are comforted by women and told that we only want to share an equal place at the table, to have a 50/50 say in important matters (pretty pretty please, daddy, can we play like the grown-ups?), we are told we've gone too far and there's a wave of backlash that attempts to rewind any progress we've made.

So when I get the question, "Why can't we just be equals?" here's how I respond: This pseudo "equality" you want always comes with a dozen stipulations to coddle men and ensure they still feel important and centered. And it does nothing to improve our safety or change patriarchal mindsets and systems set so firmly into place in the past. We are forced to play a boys' game to be granted our agency. It's conditional. But more importantly, there is no real justice or fairness in equality after patriarchy. No redress for pains and trauma. It's like a tiny Band-Aid on a stab wound through the gut, or a bit of gauze over the raw stump of a severed limb.

Furthermore, men's authority will only slow us down, creating unnecessary friction. Perhaps after women have had majority control for a good long while, then true equality could become a serious discussion. Only after we all wrap our minds around what unencumbered power and authority look like in the hands of women, and when women can walk un-afraid through the world. Until then it is neither realistic nor ethical. "Equality" is nothing short of condescending, given the demonstrable value of women and the indignities heaped upon us for all this time.

So my question for the evolved/evolving man is this. Even if you've never done any harm to any woman in your lifetime, if, individually, you have the unique opportunity to acknowledge the wounds of the past and present, to make recompense, and to set things right going forward, why then would you refuse? Aside from being a selfish myopic prick, what reason could you possibly give to walk away from doing your singular part to redress historical wrongs and facilitate true fairness? Why become a roadblock? Why would you want to withhold power and authority when it is rightfully our turn to wield it? Our turn is far overdue. It is the least you can do as a man to simply take a step back, relax, and let women drive. We could never do a worse job than men have up until now, and there's solid evidence that we can and will make some important improvements. All you have to do is get out of the way and cheer us on. Leave the table and let your sister eat her fill. And ask these same questions of the other men around you.

My sense is that the reason for any resistance is fear. Fear of a female-led world...

| 1-4 |

Fear of a Female-Led World

"Picture this: a man, let's call him Walter, contemplates the concept of gender equality. As Walter contemplates, he breaks out into a cold sweat, his heart races, his hands tremble. His imagination concocts an apocalyptic world where men are forced into submission by an army of overly-empowered, 'hysterical' women. Walter, my friend, has stumbled into the cataclysmic world of male fear of female empowerment. He's acting out a fear so irrational, so steeped in antiquated biases, that even a cursory examination of it seems like a trip through a Halloween funhouse filled with nonsensical mirrors." (Gaines)

In 1918, a program was put in place throughout the United States called the "American Plan." Federal officials began pushing every state to adopt what they called "model laws." This plan was based on similar plans implemented throughout Europe, and it lasted into the 1950s and, in some places, into the 1960s and 70s. The model laws enabled cops to arrest *any* woman suspected of having a sexually transmitted infection, subjecting her to humiliating and painful pelvic exams and S.T.I. testing. If she tested positive, she was imprisoned and treated with poisonous cures. It was a license to detain and torture women on suspicion of being sexually active. And it was not at all controversial at the time.

> *"During World War II, the American Civil Liberties Union not only failed to oppose the Plan; its founder, Roger Baldwin, sent a memorandum encouraging its local branches to cooperate with officials enforcing it. Governors and state legislatures responded to the federal government's 'model laws' with enthusiasm."*

Cops would pick women up off the streets, in most cases for no legitimate reason.

> *"Records exist in archives that document women being detained and examined for sitting at a restaurant alone; for changing jobs; for being with a man; for walking down a street in a way a male official found suspicious; and, often, for no reason at all.*
>
> *Many women were also detained if they refused to have sex with police or health officers, contemporaneous exposés*

reveal. In the late 1940s, San Francisco police officers some-times threatened to have women "vagged"—vaginally ex-amined—if they didn't accede to sexual demands. Women of color and immigrant women, in particular, were tar-geted—and subjected to a higher degree of abuse once they were locked up." (Stern)

However, the abusive authoritarian control of women's bod-ies and behavior was not a new phenomenon, and in some places, it is still accepted as normal. We need only think of the so-called honor killings that brothers and fathers dish out to sisters and daughters who have had sex outside of marriage.

The 2009 European Parliamentary Assembly had only just begun to address this issue in Resolution 1681. The resolu-tion stated:

> *"On so-called 'honor crimes,' the Parliamentary Assembly notes that the problem, far from diminishing, has wors-ened, including in Europe. It mainly affects women, who are its most frequent victims, both in Europe and the rest of the world, especially in patriarchal and fundamental-ist communities and societies. For this reason, it asked the Council of Europe member states to draw up and put into effect national action plans to combat violence against women, including violence committed in the name of so-called 'honor', if they have not already done so."*

Until the 1970s marital rape was perfectly legal in the U.S., as it was seen as a woman's duty to have sex with her husband. It wasn't until 1993 that it became illegal in all 50 states, and even now in some places, it is treated much more leniently than other kinds of sexual assault. When the person a woman is supposed to be able to trust the most violates her, it's treated as less egregious than violation by a stranger. It's remarkable that we can remain sane while immersed in such a backward culture. Women's desires and their bodily autonomy are only recently being taken into consideration at all.

Controlling women has not just been limited to sexual behaviors, either. There are many stories throughout the 20th century of women undergoing electroshock therapy for being unhappy with living a life of domestic servitude. As a result, many of these women could not count, remember people's names, or feel strong emotions at all. When women buckled under the weight of oppression, they were thought mad and subjected to further loss of freedom and harm to their person. Barring brain-damaging procedures, stressed-out moms who carried the burden of the ceaseless unpaid household labor within isolated nuclear families were hooked on Diazepam, or "Mother's Little Helper." Long-term use of the highly addictive drug causes irreversible damage to the liver and cardiovascular system and affects cognition and memory. Pop a few too many and you get deadly seizures.

On a lighter though equally disturbing note, earlier in that century, hysteria was considered a common woman's affliction, with around 75% of women said to be afflicted. The long list of potential symptoms included headache, forgetfulness, irritability, insomnia, writing cramps, hot flashes, heaviness in the limbs, usage of coarse language, difficulty breathing, desire for clitoral stimulation, hyper-promiscuity, and mood swings. It was treated by male doctors fucking patients with vibrators. At least orgasms (or "hysterical paroxysms" as the docs called them) don't come with permanent health risks.

We all know about the story of *The Scarlet Letter*. For some strange reason, teachers love to make Middle School children read that book, perhaps as an unconscious warning about how things could be again someday. But, on the subject of humiliation, need I remind you of torture devices like the Scold's Bridle used in England and Scotland a few centuries before? These were brutal iron devices attached to women's heads for the crime of talking too much or being too critical of their husbands. The contraptions often held the woman's tongue in place or pierced it with spikes. The women could be led through town by a leash attached to the bridle as a form of public humiliation. How dare she have loud opinions or bruise a man's pride!

We are more compassionate now, more enlightened. We wouldn't think of doing these things (except, of course, in some of the shady corners of the BDSM community where pathetic middle-aged men lure teenage girls into a life of being punched in the face and sexually assaulted daily as part of their "lifestyle."). But always in the back of men's minds is that thought, isn't there? What if the power dynamics were reversed? What if there was nothing to stop women from treating men as they have been treated? What if women began to think of men as objects, as property? What if, horror of horrors, men were abused with abandon, just like women were in a male-dominated society?

This is the Fear of a Woman-Led World. Power and authority are inextricable from abuse in the minds of many men. Why would anyone in power not take the opportunity to show it off in these brutal ways if they could? What would stop them? After all what else is power for if not the high of demonstrating it upon the bodies of others? Masochistic men salivate at the thought, of course, while it gives typical men a lot of anxiety. That is the patriarchal thought process. And, frankly, it's anti-feminine and ugly.

But how can I say this as a sexual sadist? Don't I also get pleasure from seeing people in pain or humiliated? Here's where I give you insight into the mind of a sadistic woman. My sadism is rooted deeply in empathy and not anxiety as it is for many men.

Freud didn't know shit about women or the female orgasm. But being a man among men, he did know a bit about the male psyche. And he had a point when he noted that the deepest fear for men is akin to castration fear, which starts as soon as he sees a member of the opposite sex naked and realizes that some people don't have a penis. It's also a fear of impotence, both physical and metaphorical. Because for patriarchal men, power is associated with force, with conquering and demonstrating their dominance in outward, showy, brutal ways, and it's all done to stave off the anxiety of someone doing the same to them. Conquer the other and you are then safe from being conquered. He must perform his dominance through force and by diminishing the power of those around him. If he can't, then he cannot feel that he has any power at all. If he's made someone writhe in pain or made them feel small and helpless, he feels protected and effective. His sadism, like his dominance, is all wrapped up in anxiety. It's wrapped up in his feelings about himself and his perceived value as a performer of action. In the patriarchal mindset, it secures his place at the top of the hierarchy.

It's worth noting, to be fair, that there are women who use sadism to gain a sense of power as well. Their numbers are far fewer, however, which is strange given how our power is stripped from us in such a systematic way. Perhaps as a group we grew accustomed to it and normalized it in ways that men don't. But the untempered female sadist can be equally brutal when compensating for her sense of helplessness. Rather than establishing and maintaining hierarchy and her place within it, the female sadist is simply grasping for a sense of freedom and control where she previously had none.

The consensually sadistic woman, however, at least from my experience in knowing quite a number of wonderfully skilled and deviant sadistic women, has a different sort of psychological make-up and a different kind of motivation. Speaking for myself, I enjoy being sadistic because of the responses in the body and mind of the person I am hurting. It's about tuning into someone and then riding their waves of sensation and emotion. My individual personality, my identity, and any ideas about myself simply evaporate. I move sadistic energy through me and into my play partner, using the constant feedback of their reactions to guide the direction of my next actions. Sadism for me is like making music, and the masochist is the instrument. It's a creative collaboration between the two of us. And without the masochist's craving for the pain and sensations I can give them, there is no desire to hurt them. With no consent, nay, with no pleading hunger coming from their end, my sadistic tendencies are neutralized.

I ran a BDSM dungeon for a few years in Chicago and had an opportunity to train dozens of women in sadomasochism. I still initiate women into the realm of BDSM through the organization I founded called the Company. And do you know what the majority of women find most difficult in the beginning? The idea of hurting someone. Until I introduce the concepts of energy exchange and go into detail about the experience and desires of the masochist and how their minds work, they are put off by the idea of exhibiting their power or authority through physical force. Only when I demonstrate that it is the ultimate game of deep, sensual, erotic empathy do they get interested and engaged in it.

There are experts in Female Led Relationships who will tell you that quite a few women are reluctant to enter into one because they don't want to become cruel or cause pain. They can't stomach the idea of brutalizing a man they care for, no matter how much it turns him on. And so the concept of "Loving FLR" - power exchange without the kink - has arisen from the needs of women who have zero interest in hurting and humiliating their men.

I do want to be clear that *all* FLR is loving FLR, even when sadomasochism is front and center as part of the dynamic. Because for the female sadist and her masochist male counterpart, S/m always serves as a point of intimate connection, both romantically and erotically. Kink erasure in the FLR community can be a bit frustrating, as the term FLR originated from within the world of BDSM. Opening that world to women for whom sadism is distasteful is fantastic. But appropriating it as strictly vanilla, and looking down on those who practice BDSM, is ignorant and problematic. As any kinkster can tell you, BDSM is an effective tool for deeper connection and sometimes for healing.

At any rate, as you read on, you will note that the Pillars of Gynarchy explicitly preclude the kind of non-consensual violations of bodily autonomy that have been commonplace within patriarchy. Over and over again I repeat my number one tenant of Gynarchy.

"The only legitimate authority is that *to which you consent* with open eyes and an open heart."

I think some men fear the specter of illegitimate authority as well as that of gender-based violence and abuse. They piss themselves at the thought of women's revenge. And it's not that the idea of revenge doesn't seem appealing and sexy to us after all we've been through. It certainly does, and we'll play those fantasies in our heads on days when men are driving us crazy. It helps us cope with the boiling rage most women feel. However, we are, quite simply put, morally better than that when it comes to constructing a world-building ideology. As I have illustrated, we have lived life on the other side of the equation. We hated it. AND WE KNOW BETTER.

And if you're not convinced of the truth in that, then let me reassure you with the fact that in Gynarchy women also create escape valves for our inevitable rageful, vengeful feelings. Remember that women deal with emotions head-on, while men repress them until they collapse or explode. We're learned emotional alchemists. The religion of Gynarchy has within it rituals of atonement which can satisfy any woman's need to punish men for all they have done, while also clearing men of any guilty feelings they may have felt as a result of both their personal and collective history. In purposeful rites, masochistic men (those fellows I mentioned before who crave and long for women's contained and directed violence) lay themselves bare to us to do as we will, so we need not take anything out on those who don't very literally beg for it. We have volunteer punching bags who are more than excited to absorb our fury and together we can spin those feelings into luxurious threads of erotic release. No man will be hurt without his enthusiastic consent.

So I ask men, what do you really have to fear? What do you have to lose? The burdens of control must have gotten heavy over the years. Don't you want to lay them down for a while? Wouldn't it be nice to follow your better nature and just take direction, and stop guessing what your place should be? Under our direction, your skills, interests, and aptitudes will be used well. They won't be wasted. We'll be your reason and motivation. Wouldn't it feel good to please women, to have women happy with you? Women can find appropriate outlets for problematic emotions, and we will not make a showy demonstration of strength by bringing the boot down on your neck (unless, of course, you like that sort of thing). We can enter an era of empathy and harmony, and you don't have to hold up that tough dominant male persona anymore. Just be useful, protective, supportive, purposeful - all the things that make men feel most fulfilled.

I have been very frank about the reasons behind Gynarchy,

and it may leave a few men feeling distraught, a bit wrung out by the realities of this dark history. You might feel men would be unwelcome or turned away in my vision of the future. But rest assured you have an important place in a woman-led world. If I thought men were not also capable of creating great beauty and utility within our communities, or if I didn't know firsthand their infinite capacity for love and devotion, I would not be writing this book. I would simply separate myself from men altogether. But I see the potential of the evolved man, and I meet men all the time who share in the goals of Gynarchy, whether they call it that or not. There are still so many left in the dark ages of zealous patriarchal dogma, but for those who have grown and continue to grow, know that I see you, and I have devoted a good deal of my life to helping you learn, improve and refine yourself in preparation for the path ahead.

PART 2

THE FOUNDATIONS

What if life as we knew it was over?
Guess what? God is a woman, I know her
What if rich, white, straight men
Didn't rule the world anymore?
(Hahahahahahahahaha)
What if rich, white, straight men
Didn't rule the world anymore?
(Hahahahahahahahaha)

Kesha, *Rich, White, Straight Men*

| 2-1 |

The Eight Pillars of Gynarchy

In part one, I established the reasons why creating Gynarchic communities is necessary. I established why patriarchy and egalitarian society should be left behind in favor of a Woman-Led World. Now it's time to get to the fun part - establishing the foundations that will provide the basis for all that comes next. The very framework of Gynarchy as an ideology.

The eight-pointed star is an almost universal symbol. It is most prominent as the symbol of the Sumerian Goddess Ishtar, later referred to as Venus. It is the Morning Star. It's seen in depictions of the Virgin Mary, and in ancient Egypt as the Ogdoad - four pairs of deities male and female. Northern Canadian Mi'kmaq Indians use the eight-pointed star pictogram on doorways and thresholds and call it Wejk-wapeniaq which in English means "the coming of the Dawn"

It's called the Kaheksakand in Estonian and is a symbol of life, fertility, and wards off evil. It represents the eight emanations of Lakshmi in Hinduism and is immediately recognizable in secular life as the compass rose.

It is light, hope, protection, and abundance - a symbol of the Divine Feminine. We use it as our guide, to show us true north, giving us a way to orient ourselves if we lose direction. Loaded with meaning, I use it here as a symbol of the Eight Pillars of Gynarchy. These are fundamental principles of any woman-led community. Our moral code.

The first Pillar, without which the whole ideology of Gynarchy risks becoming nothing more than patriarchy in reverse, is consent.

1. CONSENT

> *"There is no legitimate authority except that to which you consent with open eyes and an open heart."* (from *150 Years of Gynarchy*)

Authority without consent is tyranny, and we've been subjected to it most of our lives in the form of patriarchal religions and governments. It stomps out our intrinsic morality and deadens our internal compass. It's imposing, not welcoming. Without consent to authority, free will is a meaningless platitude.

In patriarchal religion, we are told we are inherently bad, inherently sinful. We must change to fit an unreachable ideal, a state of purity. Our desires will lead us away from conforming to the plan of an abstract "god." In Gynarchy, authenticity is paramount. If you cannot know yourself and what you want, how can you even begin to empathize with others, or understand the nature of our relationships and our very existence? We must be aware of our authentic desire (not fleeting impulses, but our true north, our heart), for it is the life force moving through us. Bypassing consent makes us soulless and mindless. It dumbs society down as a whole. It breeds anxiety and depression. How can you genuinely commit to something, how can you be devoted to someone, if you don't really want it? Devotion is not real without enthusiastic consent.

Consent to authority without manipulation or coercion is a great gift of trust. It must be given with our full awareness of both the self and the authority (open eyes) and with sweetness and surrender (an open heart). Forced authority looks pathetic and twisted in comparison. Imposed power is the disease of a ruling class unconvinced of its own credibility. Authority without consent breeds contempt and resentment, or at best limp heartless compliance. It does not connect the ruling and the ruled in a dance of symbiosis, it puts a wall between them.

Consent can be given in broad strokes as with blanket consent or given with conditions. And it can be withdrawn at any time if the trust required is broken. In this way, it holds authority accountable to that over which it rules. It's a built-in mechanism to topple tyranny before it gets a foothold.

2. BODILY AUTONOMY

Along with consent comes bodily autonomy. It is patriarchy's peculiar fixation to monitor, manage and control women's bodies. Our bodies are the one possession that comes with us throughout our lives. Most humans are heavily identified with our bodies. We shape them, change them, and decorate them. We put them through tests of stress and strain and find out just how resilient they can be. We should get to know our bodies intimately and learn what they need and care for these amazing flesh machines better than any other object. Everything else is replaceable.

The human body is miraculous. It contains a human brain which is a device more sophisticated than any computer and has the ability to give us access to knowledge quite literally beyond reason. We each get only one. To think that one is owed the use of someone else's body is the worst kind of arrogance. Just like consent, if someone wants to give you use of their body because they desire it or feel it is right, then one should take it as a gift unlike any other.

Autonomy in the most basic sense means self-governance, or the ability to make decisions for oneself. However, to philosopher Immanuel Kant, autonomy is the individual's capacity to act according to an objective morality and not just according to his own whims. Autonomy is the ability to control ourselves, but also to have self-control in a way that allows us to act in the way we know is right. We put our bodies to tasks that we feel will be best for us and for our society as a whole. Autonomy need not always be self-centered. Freedom is also to be free from impulsive internal forces that might lead us away from our core values. In terms of bodily autonomy, we deserve to be free of addiction and compulsions that block us from being the best and most morally attuned versions of ourselves.

Try to remember that if you find you drink too much or smoke too much weed and get hazy, or if you load up on sugary sweets. Think of the man who engages in cheating or breaks the bonds of a consensual contract between him and his partner, and then says that he just could not help himself. Doing those things just because you felt compelled to in the moment is not true bodily autonomy, because you're being ruled over by your fleeting impulses.

The Gynarchist knows the value of clearly communicated agreement taken seriously. Pledges and contracts are our tools to help maintain autonomy, to articulate our needs and core desires, and reinforce them when we forget. It also prevents our boundaries and limits from being trampled. And with continual communication, these agreements can be modified and amended as we move forward and grow.

3. COLLABORATION

Competition may be fun when taken lightly, as sport. But the one quality of the human race that has enabled us to survive for as long as we have is collaboration. We need one another. The sooner we acknowledge it and begin taking others' needs as seriously as our own, working toward mutually beneficial goals, the more readily we can advance as a species.

> *"If we Homo sapiens want to continue our fascinating, yet so far relatively short, evolutionary success story, we have to evolve wise societies characterized by empathy, solidarity and collaboration. Wise cultures are regenerative and protect bio-cultural diversity as a source of wealth and resilience* (Wahl)*."*

In the backward world of patriarchal capitalism, "Fuck you I've got mine," is the common refrain. Competition is seen as a prime motivator for progress. Isolation, as rugged individuals or singular nuclear family units is the norm. And it is killing us.

In the 19th and 20th centuries, the view was that competition was born of scarcity. Maybe in desperate situations that's true. But the oversimplification of "survival of the fittest," meant we are all just looking out for our own in a world of lack. We are now beginning to realize that the reverse is true. This planet has an abundance of resources that, if managed well, could provide for all of us. Scarcity, it turns out, must be artificially manufactured to perpetuate the drive for competition. Patriarchy warps the narrative to suit a more masculine disposition.

It has been observed by those who study human social systems and biology that women are generally more collaborative as a group than men. We tend to take the concerns of those around us into consideration and work toward win-

win situations and a harmony of needs and desires. There's a reason they call compulsive competition a dick-measuring contest. Men took the childish game of comparisons and made it their M.O. But their hormones are at least partially to blame.

> *"On average, women release Oxytocin more than men. Men release more Testosterone than women and it competes with Oxytocin, so Oxytocin can be stifled. Oxytocin shuts down under high stress and extreme competition. One stimulates competition while the other stimulates collaboration and co-operation. As Ken Nowack of Envisia Learning observes:*
>
> *Zak's findings support the observation that women tend to release more oxytocin than men, thus they directly contribute more empathy, cooperation and trust in interpersonal interactions. These hormonal differences might help explain the observed tendency for women to deploy more participative leadership behaviors relative to their male counterparts and naturally use transformational practices that emphasize teamwork, cooperation, networking and interpersonal support."*

Given that men stripped us of autonomy, women fell into the competitive patriarchal trap in one obvious respect. We became dependent, required to attach ourselves to men in order to survive, and so we had to compete for men's approval. That worked out great for men, of course, in terms of squeezing whatever uses they wanted out of us and keeping us under control. But as the yoke of dependence is being lifted from our shoulders, more and more women are realizing how humiliating that really was. And we're done. We're demeaned and exhausted from going against our collaborative nature and being competitive pick-me-ass bitches (PMABs in colloquial terms). That era is coming to an end. We are now painfully conscious of our knee-jerk back-biting responses to one another instilled in us by our mothers or grandmothers and we talk through it. We are once again returning to the comfort of the bosom of sisterhood. As the feminine consciousness evolves, hurting another woman to gain a man's attention becomes downright pathetic.

A Feminine style of relationships and leadership is beginning to be recognized as effective, even within classically patriarchal systems like business. We are in a transitional period wherein organizations are rethinking old biases.

> "We found showing sensitivity and concern for others—stereotypically feminine traits—made someone less likely to be seen as a leader. However, it's those same characteristics that make leaders effective. Thus, because of this unconscious bias against communal traits, organizations may unintentionally select the wrong people for leadership roles, choosing individuals who are loud and confident but lack the ability to support their followers' development and success." (Gaskell)

The Pillars of Gynarchy bring humans closer together for our collective fulfillment. We acknowledge our interconnectedness. Competition tends to separate us. And so in Gynarchy, a bias in favor of collaboration is only natural.

4. ABUNDANCE

Are you aware of how retail stores will damage unsold merchandise, painting or cutting brand new clothes, shoes, and other products just so they cannot be salvaged by scavengers and dumpster divers? You can be arrested for digging through retail garbage in some places, but there are no penalties for destroying twenty pairs of perfectly good sneakers and sending them to the landfill. The bean counters have figured out that such "losses" are better for the company's bottom line than making charitable donations.

Do you know how much food is thrown out by our expansive supermarkets, or by farmers when stores keep bidding under cost for their produce for so long that it rots in heaps? Have you ever been to a garbage dump, and seen the mounds of waste? Not just bags of common household trash but furniture, electronics, and appliances? Do you know about the shops overseas where low-wage workers risk their health to extract precious metals from our refuse? We throw away more value in a year than those workers could consume in their lifetimes.

We produce so much more than we need in every aspect of life, yet some people go without basic necessities. This is just the result of inefficient and haphazard resource management which has plagued us since the industrial revolution and before. And the driving forces behind this waste are competition and greed.

Patriarchal capitalism invented artificial scarcity. We have more than enough, but a handful of people are going to lock it all up behind paywalls. The CEO of the company Nestlé even wants to take control of water. These corporations simply toss out the excess if it can't grow their bank accounts. Excess that required raw materials and labor to produce. All of that, wasted.

How is it not a crime that one person has more money than they could spend in 100 lifetimes, while whole families struggle to pay for housing and utilities? Billionaires could help solve world hunger and homelessness, but they won't. Because they somehow see themselves as deserving of and entitled to the abundance created by their workers' labor, upon whose backs they built their fortunes, more than the workers themselves. The only difference between you and a billionaire is that they don't care how many people they exploit. The myth that they work harder than you is absolute bunk. They simply convince others to do the work for them as cheaply as possible. And to admire that kind of sociopathy as "success" is to buy into the brainwashing and lose connection to your humanity. As human beings go, billionaires are miserable failures. They are nothing more than hoarders.

Nature provides us with nonstop solar, wind, and hydro-electric sources of power. When managed properly, agriculture is a freely available self-perpetuating resource to feed us all. Plants make the seeds to keep growing more plants. The soil regenerates its own nutrients by incorporating decaying matter. This planet is rich! What happens when humans abandon an area? Nature envelopes that area in rich, lush growth teaming with life!

We are the only animals on earth who have to pay rent or mortgages, though nature provides us with the raw materials to build shelter. Raw materials that also build the tens of thousands of houses that sit unused and empty in this country. More waste.

> *"We should do away with the absolutely specious notion that everybody has to earn a living. It is a fact today that one in ten thousand of us can make a technological breakthrough capable of supporting all the rest."* Buckminster Fuller

We could all live in abundance. We now have the knowledge and technology to do everything efficiently and sustainably, with minimal waste, and provide for everyone. We just choose not to. Because not doing so keeps the market competitive. We are taught from birth that it's our duty to add value to corporate shareholders' lives and financial portfolios, and yet they are under no obligation to return the favor.

Our communities must be acutely aware of this and do all we can to reverse it. We must not fear lack nor live yoked to the anxiety that drives hoarding. We must use human intellect and innovation in concert with nature to maximize sustainability, not profit. **The profit motive is the enemy of abundance.** When humans come together and pool our resources and begin to create new resources through our collective efforts, no one goes hungry. This is how we were able to survive and evolve in the first place. The more we give to and share with one another, the less survival stress we are all subjected to, and the more we have in terms of the human capacity to create and cultivate abundance.

And before the words leave your lips, this is not "Marxism." This is Gynarchy. Don't make the mistake of giving a man credit for what women have always known. Think of a woman's breasts, so naturally filling with all the sustenance needed to feed the being that she grew within her. Women are naturally regenerative and sustainable. Our very bodies are abundance personified.

5. NETWORKS

You know about the Internet, but have you heard of the "Wood Wide Web?" A tree looks like an independent majestic thing that stands alone. But in reality, under our feet, trees are in regular communication with other trees across vast landscapes in a web of mycorrhiza - "fungus root." In a symbiotic relationship, fungi feed trees nutrients and in turn, receive nourishment from the trees' photosynthesis. Through fungal threads, trees also send and receive resources such as sugars and carbon from one another and send messages about potential dangers such as insect invasions. Trees can even send chemical messages to animals, like hungry birds, to help them when they are overrun with damaging bugs. In forests, nodes called "Mother Trees" standing tall and reaching toward the sun send carbon to younger trees that are under the shade of the canopy overhead, unable to catch direct sunlight. Dying trees can disperse their carbon to their living cousins across the network.

As a young woman in college studying philosophy and social sciences, I became enamored with the idea of the rhizome as an alternative to hierarchy. Rhizomes are common among grasses and send root systems underground capable of popping up and propagating whole new plants in new locations. It's a way of organizing life horizontally, with multiple connected points, not in a top-heavy pyramid. It seems so natural, and so in tune with the design of the universe.

Lines should vibrate and connect, not block and divide. Remember, everything in Gynarchy is about interconnectedness.

Borders may prevent the crossing of humans from one place to another, but they don't prevent the crossing of any other life. Not birds, nor bees, not the seeds and roots of plants, nor even the communication of individual free-standing trees. Borders may at one time have been lines drawn on paper by map makers demarcating the more or less natural divisions in the landscape. But the way in which they are believed in as real and heavily policed now, they've become unnecessary and artificial walls, perpetuated, like most patriarchal concepts, out of anxiety. Borders speak of fear. They say, "Gotta protect what's mine."

Nationalism is a mental illness. When one suffers from it, it has the effect of making other humans seem alien and threatening. It causes the afflicted to judge others on arbitrary criteria like location or language. It creates delusions of superiority. It is a contagion that slips into the psyche through positive feelings of pride and then covertly infects its host with paranoia, hostility, and aggression. It is the cause of both discrimination within borders (against immigrants - the other) and war between geographic neighbors.

Networks morph and expand, always finding new trajectories. It is an outward movement that seeks not to conquer but to share and include. If you've ever watched a murmuration of starlings, you can see the beauty and synchrony of a network in motion. Each individual bird pays attention to the movements of the seven birds closest to her, and together they orchestrate breathtaking shapes that swoop and float across the sky. Networks are not rigid and divisive. Like those of starlings, human networks are shifting, adapting, changing, and ever alive. Gynarchy is a network, always seeking new connections and inviting new nodes.

6. THE HIVE

Networks are made up of nodes and within Gynarchy I call these nodes Hives. I use the imagery of the beehive because bees have survived 30 million years, 5 times longer than homo sapiens, and the shape of their societies has not changed much over time. In hives, the members all strive to support the hive as a whole, and their motivation at the center of it all is the Queen. The Queen sets up camp and the hive forms around her. Move the Queen and the hive follows. She is the central symbolic and practical focus that holds the hive together. Their raison d'être.

Bees are also known as not only a sustainable species but an ULTRA sustainable species. That means they provide more value to the environment than they take from it. In gathering their nectar, they pollinate plants, assuring more than enough plant life to sustain their needs and that of other animals. And with their excess food production, they provide us with their delicious honey. Bees are a symbol of sweet abundance.

And though the comparison has been made to systems like monarchy, bees don't reflect a hierarchy. It is said that no bee starves unless the whole hive starves. Each and every member of the hive has an important role, and each and every member of the hive is cared for just as they all care for the Queen.

Their communication methods are also quite efficient. When delivering messages via their vibrations and dances they do it in such a way that it effectively tags only those bees who need the information, the others then know the message does not pertain to them and their work is undisturbed by it. Bees also create elaborate "phone trees" of pheromones with messages passed from hive to hive to lead lost bees back home to their Queen. After 30 million years, they've got it all down to a fine art. Isn't it telling then, that only recently, at the peak of the reign of patriarchy when monoculture and pesticides and lawns grown for status encroach upon the previous more organic farming methods, our human presence threatens their survival? It threatens our survival as well.

At any rate, the hive model with its central female leader (or small group of female leaders, depending upon the size) is the structure of the individual communities within the Gynarchic network. These are individual sects within the wider religion. Each woman who wishes to lead makes herself known and gathers others around her who will live to serve her unifying vision. She provides the purpose and the focus around which others can contribute their efforts in their particular roles. And the Queen's job is to provide authority - that is to be the author of the story and the designer of the shape of her community, and to connect and communicate with other Queens to share knowledge and resources.

The Queen does not become Queen for status, nor for attention, nor for wealth, although one or more of those things may come with the job. The Queen becomes Queen because she thinks about the big picture and knows what a thriving hive will look like - one that is beneficial for all members. She becomes Queen out of her heartfelt desire to lead. Others trust her judgment enough to surround her, support her, and serve her goals. Each hive will be different, attuned to the desires and personality of the Queen, and some may even have a pair or a small group of Queens who share a common vision. Women within the hive may use their first hive as a training ground and later branch off and build their own in the future. This prevents hives from becoming too large and unmanageable. And since other hives are automatically seen as collaborators and nodes in the same network rather than competitors, battles between hives would be almost unthinkable.

7. CONFLICT RESOLUTION

There's a Canadian relationship coach named Chantal Heide who teaches that a "no fight relationship" is the goal for long-term intimate partners. This sometimes befuddles those who come into her live streams online. How can any two people live together and never fight? She says that if you lay the groundwork in the beginning of the relationship, know who you are getting involved with well before getting serious, and confirm that they meet your predetermined criteria for what you want in the relationship, then there may be some disagreements, but they will never devolve into yelling and fights. Shouting matches and threatening behavior should never be tolerated. If a man doesn't meet your criteria over a three-month vetting period, then move on. Having too many points of incompatibility between you is just trouble waiting to happen.

This works well for dating and romantic relationships, and particularly for FLR, where the woman's desires are centered. But we can't make sure everyone we encounter in life meets our requirements for harmonious communication, and depending upon the situation, dismissing them and moving on is not always an option.

"Don't win fights, win allies," says Kasia Urbaniak, a women's power coach. In her classes, she teaches about the importance of locating and approving of someone with whom you are in a disagreement. This means confirming with them that what you hear them saying is accurate and empathizing with them before presenting a conflicting point. Only then can you influence them and help them see your point of view. Everyone likes to know that they've been heard, understood and that the opposing party has empathy for them. Connection, not division, is the way of Gynarchy.

Beyond one-to-one relationships, how would the Gynarchist leader avoid things like war? I like to point out that Gynarchists are actively, not passively, anti-war. One way to avoid war is to avoid conquering or encroaching upon the free will of others. The Gynarchist has no use for colonization. Gynarchy draws people in through attraction and invitation, it doesn't go around imposing itself. There should be no revolt from within our communities since we hold fast to the pillars of consent and bodily autonomy. And because Gynarchy is predicated on networks and not borders, and the coexistence of different groups with differing ideologies is not resisted, but accepted as normal, there is less reason for violence to erupt. We value authenticity. We're not butting heads with other groups. We don't make any attempt to forcibly convert them to our way of life. It's a very live-and-let-live approach.

That eliminates at least 50% of the reason for going to war with another group. We don't go around starting fights, stealing land and property, or hurting others. In fact, we should be available to help others refine their own communities, advise and solve problems through education if asked. Knowledge should be freely shared.

But what if someone tries to encroach upon our communities? What if some other group wants to start trouble with us? First, we call upon our network of support to exert pressure from the outside and to collaborate on solutions. Gather witnesses to the conflict. When it's clear that our small communities are not vulnerable and alone, it reduces the appeal of bullying.

Secondly, we find out what the need or want of the other group is. There is usually some underlying motive. We locate and approve of it, just like in interpersonal conflict. We determine why they are on the attack, and how we can resolve or mitigate any aggravating factors. People will attack either what they don't understand or what they feel threatened by. Both of those motivations are reasonably easy to remedy through connection and discussion.

So what's left is the tiny percentage of groups and people who will attack because they are intrinsically aggressive and wish to conquer someone. First, you must infiltrate the group and find out if all members are in agreement with senseless escalation. Chances are you'll discover some dissent, some who feel their voices are not being heard, and the dissenters are the ones you want to get close to. Find potential allies within.

And at last, if all else fails, be prepared to put up a strong defense and gather round all those willing to help. In the process, you will have been getting to know your opponents inside and out, trying to understand what makes them tick. Find their vulnerabilities and fight smart, not hard. Every group has its weaknesses, and those with the conqueror mentality are not that sophisticated to begin with. Their competitiveness and need for ego validation will likely be an Achilles heel.

In the midst of battle, minimize harm so as not to breed contempt and resentment among those more neutral. Maintain a reputation for compassion. Turn people. Make being a prisoner of our side more pleasant than being a soldier for the opposition. Deprogram any zealots. With our immense capacity for empathy, Gynarchists should become adept at intense psychological warfare as a means of self-defense. Use manipulation over physical violence. Mind fuck techniques can be far more effective than brute force.

It is important for women to know some form of violent self-defense to use in a pinch. But if ever we have the need to turn to serious physical warfare, we should employ the Feminine art of Witchcraft. Like the ancient Witch Goddess Circe, we can make ourselves familiar with the catalogues of pharmacopeia - plant medicine. Turn the tables with intoxicants, sedatives, mood enhancers, laxatives, hypnotics, hormone disruptors, and psychedelics, all delivered discreetly through touch or food, or helpfully carried on the elements, in the air and water. Any combination of those is effective at neutralizing aggression. Remember to fight like a woman.

Always keep in mind, however, that the ultimate goal is never to have to fight at all. The ideal is to create allies, not enemies, even in times of conflict. And doing so can be as simple as never encroaching upon others' free will and letting people be. Draw close to us those who are capable of harmonious relations and share knowledge and goodwill. Be selective in our communities making sure that all members understand and are attuned to our ideology. Those who adamantly reject our ways can be left to their own devices. In conflict, use empathy as a superpower, figure out the underlying motivations and needs, and treat the source not just the symptoms of aggression.

8. THE FEMININE AS DIVINE

"To the Queen of Heaven, The Goddess of the Universe, the One who walked in terrible Chaos and brought life by the Law of Love; And out of Chaos brought us harmony,

and from Chaos Thou has led us by the hand." Babylon, Eighteenth to Seventeenth Century, BCE.

In the beginning, woman was god. Every one of us, every living human being, cannot enter this earthly realm but through the body of a female. A woman is literally your creator. Before formula and baby bottles, women's breasts kept us alive until we were able to eat solid food. They magically concoct the perfect sustenance for the growing baby, adjusting to their individual dietary needs.

But beyond the physical manifestation, if we look to the religions predating Abraham and his jealous god (jealous of whom, I wonder?), on the Indian continent, the Feminine, as a more abstract concept called Shakti, is known as the energy that creates all things from the silent nothingness. It was Her desire to know Herself that created binaries and then ever-unfolding multiplicity.

When the Feminine is acknowledged as divine - as the source - women are protected, cherished, and sacred. They are central to life's meaning. They are powerful, their will to create unhampered. Harmony and beauty exist for all when the force of creation is not blocked or locked away. We cultivate abundance.

When the Feminine is maligned both women and men suffer. Power turns perverse and anxious. Fear, competition, and comparison are used to control. Fingers are pointed at anyone who lives fearlessly and doesn't conform as the source of all woes. There is nothing left to do but conquer and hoard in an attempt to relieve the anxiety, to serve the need to feel that man's existence is justified and important. He becomes disconnected from his source, lost in struggle. The patriarchal man may be terrified of hell, though he himself has created it for himself and for those around him.

In pagan times religion was a connection to nature, religion was philosophy, religion was culture, and religion was therapy before therapy existed. Religious adherents passed down knowledge about the origins and nature of our existence, about how we may know ourselves. Religion has been the glue of societies and helped those in chaos find purpose and meaning in life. And so it is with the tool of religion that we build this movement. But it must be a religion that proclaims what we knew before that knowledge became shamed and repressed - that the Feminine is divine.

...

These eight pillars are the foundation and framework of any Gynarchic community. You may note that the metaphors I use to help describe these pillars exist in nature, as Gynarchy is a natural and Earth-based system. We realize that humanity is an integral part of nature, not its master, nor its foe.

With each scaffolding in place, we can build a million variations of society on a small scale and link them up through this common ideology, each new iteration adding knowledge and resources to the rest. Every new success will open the eyes of others to see what is possible. No aggressive or bloody revolution will be needed, just the growth of interconnected and related systems that work better than the patriarchy. The lifecycle of the male-dominated paradigm is coming to an inevitable end.

The details of each community can be guided by Feminine Principles. To understand what that looks like, we must understand what "The Feminine" really is. But first, I feel I cannot ignore a timely topic that has surfaced as the hold of patriarchy is weakening, and which generates a lot of discussion in both academic and mainstream social circles. That topic is the gender binary.

| 2-2 |

The Gender Binary

In my mind, I can hear the critique from my own gender-fluid child upon reading this book. At a young age, with no prompting from their clearly Gynarchist Mama, the child I thought was my daughter declared that they had no allegiance to the binary and instead would float among and between gender identities however they saw fit whenever they saw fit. Given my gender-dependent ideology, you may be surprised that, though I was initially taken aback, I'm perfectly OK with it. In fact, I like how it has broadened my perspective, and how it makes me have to think critically about every gendered idea that I espouse.

If you are anything like my kiddo, up 'til now you might think with all my talk of the differences between women and men and all these binary comparisons between patriarchy and Gynarchy, that I'm ignoring the elephant in the room. What about the sizable minority of people who don't fit that binary? And where do trans folk belong in all of this?

Whenever a concept is born, its opposite is also born simultaneously. To know what a man is we must also know what he is not. Most obviously, he is not a woman. But the concept of "the opposite of that" is not the only thing sharing that moment of concept creation. We also give birth to three more concepts that are "not that thing." There is the thing and its opposite, and then there is also 1.) the conceptually related thing which is neither, 2.) the conceptually related thing which is both, and 3.) the thing which floats between, taking on the qualities of each of the opposing concepts at different times. This *transitional* concept can move permanently from one opposite state to another, or continually move back and forth in a fluid manner.

For example, if you have a hot water tap and a cold water tap, by running both at different volumes you also create cool or lukewarm temperatures. You can turn off the water if you like, and you can also easily switch between the two taps at different times and still get wet. The binary of hot and cold is still quite real. By naming hot, we then had to name cold in contrast. The opposites always exist, but there are also nuances that land just outside of and in between them. This is true of most pairs of opposites - left/right, up/down, backward/forward, good/bad.

As I teach in the chapter on biology, first there was the female, and from there, a mutation evolved to help us diversify our genes. We call that mutation male. And so, social systems clung to our biological differences, and the sex-based gender binary was established in a time so long ago we can barely imagine it. It was used to decide the distinct division of labor and power. A simple observation of opposites was made prescriptive and political, and it has been that way ever since. And it wasn't long before transgender, non-binary, and gender-fluid nuances became points of resistance. They stand as ways to subvert the hold of the unearned authority of male dominance and above all else, to embrace authenticity in contrast to social conformity.

In 2022, patriarchy-loving right-wing pundit Matt Walsh wrote an entire feature-length documentary titled "What is a Woman?" His point was not to answer that question, exactly, but to paint gender theory as madness and transgender people as "groomers" who are indoctrinating children into a perverse cult. You know, doing basically what his religion of Christianity has normalized as righteous and good when it comes to their own belief system. In psychoanalysis that's known as "projection."

His pretense of open-mindedness was a goofy farce. It was a passionate but ignorant bit of propaganda. And it inspired me to try to answer that question for myself. "What is a woman?" is, in fact, a great question, and an important one if one is attempting to justify an entire ideology based on an unequal power dynamic between the two predominant genders.

I felt my definition of woman should be both well-reasoned and inclusive. Matt's final answer "adult human female," was too redundant, and not at all comprehensive.

Let me break it down: The answer is that it is *not* just the presence of primary or secondary female sex traits. To suggest a woman is solely defined by being a baby maker or having a vagina and tits is pretty insulting. A woman who can't give birth, or who lives without a uterus or breasts, or even without a vagina is not LESS of a woman. Nor is her gender just defined by social expression. It's not pretty dresses or effete mannerisms. Not all women express womanness (womanhood?) in the same style of clothing or hair or even the way they move or talk.

Woman is definitely a purely human-made concept used for the convenience of classification (frankly, we could have just as easily established strict social norms based on height or birth month), but it also has real and lasting consequences in terms of how other humans treat us, our rights, roles, etc. Gender is constructed, yes, but you can't get around the fact that it is also quite real and important to how humans operate in the world. So what it boils down to is an identity. And identities are based on a number of factors and are not dependent on any one thing alone. You certainly don't have to check off every box in the woman column (neither biologically nor socially) in order to be considered "woman."

It's not a new concept. I call it constellation theory. There are things we associate with women which include modes of social expression, biology, ways of seeing and thinking about the world, and intrinsic feelings (that internal sense that "I am a woman."). All of these are points in a constellation. Some of these points change over time or differ from culture to culture. With enough corresponding points in the "woman zone," you are a woman. That means there are feminine-appearing women with penises and masculine-appearing women with vaginas. There are women who give birth and women who don't. There are women who shop for clothes in the men's section of the store and men who like to wear lace panties. And there are women who start life as boys. Those are called trans women. They aren't cis-gendered women, and they don't have the same experiences of gender as us, but they are a type of woman.

This definition is so nuanced that the simpleminded get confused, thinking that it means anyone can legitimately call themselves a woman. I disagree. No one point is mandatory to be a woman, but it does require one having a majority of points within the woman constellation to make it true. Otherwise, the definition itself is meaningless. Some people have a greater number of characteristics in the category of man, and some people are simply the epitome of balance and are therefore more androgynous.

When I first started thinking about the question "What is a woman?" I was less analytic about it and waxed poetic.

"A woman is whatever the fuck she wants to be," is always my snarky answer. But my heart says:

> *I want to sing the praises of women and pour my heart out. Women, the Feminine (capital F), feminine energy as I see it, is that which creates the whole of existence and that without which nothing could exist. Masculine energy is simply inert without feminine energy. And in the human form of that vibration turned to matter, men without women are, to be honest, kind of pointless as a category. I am sure many would disagree with that vehemently, but it's my feeling, nonetheless. And I do not say that with any*

hatred or lack of care for men. It's just that we are essential to their continued existence, and they should know that.

To be a woman is to be a being with superpowers, within a category of fellow beings full of magic. Without us, the human world would end. Within us resides the knowledge of creation and destruction. And by that, I don't just mean physical reproduction. That is only a small piece of the puzzle. I don't feel it's hyperbole to say being a woman is the highest form of being human. To put it in less hierarchical terms, we are the basis and the essence of humanity.

As a result of that magic and ultra-relevance and the anxiety it may inspire, being a woman comes with a great deal of bullshit and baggage. It comes with oppression and suppression of our innate power and our innate and endless variety of expressions, archetypes, and continuous living innovations in identity itself. It comes with narrow social expectations, abuse, repression, objectification, and much too much psychological and physical violence heaped upon us just for being women.

It's painful. It's enough to make one reject woman-ness as a curse. But we are not the roles and attitudes imposed upon us and we never have been. I feel like we are slowly waking to the reality that we, collectively, can reset the direction of life on Earth. And only as women and women's magic could. Where there is strife, we can create cooperation.

Where there are wounds, we can heal. With solidarity and an acknowledgment of our shared struggles, we can reclaim ourselves as Goddesses on earth, celebrating each other. And we should understand with humility the kind of weight that collective reclamation carries. The kind of world-building change that it initiates. At times it will look like burning it all down.

And so we must treat each other with tender care and understanding of the turmoil that happens as we burn. Look with adoring eyes at our missteps and stumbles. None of this is easy, but given the right circumstances, it can create ease.

This is what my heart is saying loud and clear. What is a woman? A woman is catalyst and creator, growth and decay, love and rage, alchemist and garden vine, twisting and turning to find the right light. And lastly, men can be the supporting trellis or the raw material from which we invent the universe again.

Though wistfully emotional, I think that's still a much better answer than the dully robotic "adult human female" response of the patriarchs, don't you? And no one can take the magic of being born into womanhood away from us simply by existing as something different. Even less so by embracing the womanly qualities in themselves. So let's return to the question of the gender binary, and its outliers.

In ancient Mesopotamia, the Goddess Inanna (aka, Ishtar) had priests and priestesses who were pansexual and trans-gendered. Enheduanna, High Priestess of the Moon in the Sumerian city of Ur wrote that the Goddess had the power to turn men into women and women into men. It was not taboo, and never profane.

Throughout history and across cultures there have always been examples of a "third gender" or even multiple genders, such as the six genders listed in the Jewish Talmud. From the Hijra in India to the Bissu in Indonesia, people who either transition genders or exist between genders are given ded-icated spiritual roles, perform blessings and rituals, and are given a special place in each society. They are seen as having a unique perspective, both feminine and masculine. They are sometimes seen as bridging the gap between the worldly and the divine. These nuances of gender have *always* existed since the idea of gender was born, and they have even been celebrated. I don't understand why some folks are suddenly so bothered by them now.

The only arguments I hear to the contrary of acceptance and celebration are rooted in fear and anxiety. Trans Ex-clusionary Radical Feminists fear that it gives men a covert way to talk over us, steal energy away from feminist voices, or invade and infiltrate our exclusive spaces. To that I say, in a woman-led world all spaces are women's spaces. When one owns the whole house, one need not pine for a room of one's own. In Gynarchy *all* conversations respect the needs and desires of women, and we are heard when we speak. When we are powerful, protected, and free, the anxiety over being overpowered, invaded, and negated by men will sub-side. Within feminism we must fight for every tiny scrap of authority and safety we can get inside the patriarchal construct. In Gynarchy, this is not the case. And furthermore, basing womanhood on biology alone is to define ourselves in the way patriarchy always has - as a womb and a pussy to fuck. The whole anti-trans argument is nothing more than a well-disguised misogynistic trap, baited with women's unmet need for safety.

In Gynarchy, authenticity is paramount. Knowing who you truly are and what role you play in your community is essential to your own fulfillment. I see no reason why a Gynarchist would reject the legitimacy of transwomen or those who are fluid or non-binary. Their existence does not negate our own womanhood, nor does it erase the binary itself. I don't mean to sound smug when I say that even the concept of non-binary is dependent upon the existence of the binary, without which it would simply disappear. It's important, rather than getting caught up in the implications of the exceptions, to step back and see what's really there. In reality, women and men who identify as one or the other are still the majority, and I doubt that will change soon. We can still promote and live by the authority of women in women-led hives and networks while respecting the existence of fluid and non-binary folks and welcoming them within our communities. In a woman-led world, trans and non-binary people should have unique roles as they always have, as natural connectors - bridges between perspectives and worlds.

| 2-3 |

The Nature of The Feminine

Gynarchy is an ideology built on feminine principles, and not necessarily female genitals.

I see a lot of talk about femininity and the Feminine, of "coming into your feminine," and feminine energy. And what I notice most is that a lot of people get this wrong. They are leaning on patriarchal models that men have put in place to cultivate something or someone easy to control and dismiss. A not-quite-equal counterbalance to the masculine.

So what is the Feminine, really? And what in the world do I mean when I talk about feminine principles and feminine energy?

I have been known to tell my students, "We are all just Devi playing with Herself."

First, the Feminine (capital F) is not one side of a duality or polarity. It has no equal opposite. With all you may have heard both from Abrahamic religion and the New Age movement, this revelation could come as some surprise.

Put simply, The Feminine (known as Shakti or Devi) is the vibration that turns silence into sound, and nothingness into something. It is the energy that creates matter, time, and even thought.

There exists the vast ocean of silent, unmoving, unmanifest potential (sometimes called Siva/Shiva). That is the place we humans attempt to dive into when we sit and meditate. We follow vibration to its most subtle and refined state until we reach the end where there is only "that which is not" - the literal definition of Siva. It is endlessly vast and deep. It is not active but simply exists. It is presence. It has no defining characteristics, no shape, no movement.

It was in the moment that this vast silent potential desired to know and understand "what am I?" that The Feminine (Devi/Shakti) emerged as that which causes everything to exist. It is nothing less than the original vibration and impulse of life itself. The Mother of all things that, from Herself, gave birth to all duality and all multiplicity. There is no separate and equal consort. Siva (Unmanifest Potential) and Shakti (the Feminine or Devi which creates) are not two opposite ideas but one singular wholeness existing both in the state of stillness and the state of vibration simultaneously. This is described as non-duality.

From the Feminine the masculine was created, not as an equal but as a manifestation made of Her and for Her.

The oldest known creation myth in history reflects this. In the Pelasgian myth, The Goddess of all things emerges from chaos and first divides the sky from the sea, the above from below. In other words, She creates duality. Then from the north wind that follows from Her movements as She dances on the water, She fashions the serpent. The serpent follows Her, observing Her, tracing Her every move, wrapping round Her limbs. She had manifested a necessary witness to Her being. The serpent is the knowledge of "What am I?" The serpent is so moved and so enamored by Her that it makes love to Her. Afterward, She assumes the form of a dove, and She births the egg of the universe. She bids the serpent to coil around the egg and the egg cracks and hatches and from it emerges all we can see, experience, and know in this universe.

To reiterate, the Goddess, emerging from chaos, created duality in order to know that She exists as something, rather than nothing. She created a witness fashioned from the wind of Her movement to get to know *what* She is. She then got jiggy with that witness, who was the embodied knowledge of "what am I" in the form of a serpent studying Her every move, and thus created everything in the universe.

In the myth, She then rests at the top of the highest mountain and the serpent follows. As they look out observing all that is, the serpent says "Wow, look at what *I* created!"

claiming authorship of the universe. And with that, Devi kicks out his teeth and banishes him from the mountain. One of his teeth becomes the first man.

It kind of puts the whole serpent in the garden story into a very different perspective, doesn't it? And it explains why the serpent image has always been associated with the Goddess and the Divine Feminine. And it's also why the Naga - the semi-divine race of serpents in Hinduism - are the ones who lead humans to knowledge. It all seems to stem from that original explanation of source and creation.

And in a future chapter, I can show how the mythology aligns with our current understanding of biology - that the female existed first, and the male was a useful mutation that came after. With this foundational understanding in place, it's clear how the view of the Feminine as the passive half of an equal and balanced duality is an egregious misunderstanding. There are lots of dualities in existence. Devi cannot know Herself without causing duality, without having opposites to compare (as well as nuances between opposites). But the Divine Feminine is without equal.

So what is feminine energy? What are feminine qualities? How does one get in touch with femininity?

First and foremost, the fundamental nature of the Feminine is **creative**. She loves variety and will endlessly create new combinations and variations. You can see that in music and art, and in the variety of animals, plants, and human bodies and faces. She is experimentation, innovation, and growth.

She creates beauty and awe. Just look at the variety of sea creatures alone as a testament to Her endless imagination.

She is **abundant**. You may have heard the saying that if you give a woman something good, She will multiply it. This is the nature of the Feminine. She is bursting with more and more.

She is **cyclical**. Tied to the moon phases and women's menstrual cycles, the Feminine is a spiral of endless cycles through time. Birth, growth, death, decay, and rebirth are Her patterns. Nothing is wasted. Decay feeds new life, life reproduces, regenerating itself.

She is **playful**. Like Lila, the Indic concept of the universe as a playground of the divine. She speaks in metaphors, stories, and double entendre. She will trick you, not to harm you but to see how you respond. She's a mad scientist. Laugh and play back and life will be blissful and great fun. She does not want you to get bogged down, but instead to cleverly find your way out of Her traps. Do so and you'll find rewards. She craves engagement and entertainment. She loves collaboration and all the novel new variations that emerge from combining one thing or one person with another. Life is a game. She laughs in glee at its absurdity.

She is **active**. Far from the passive feminine of patriarchal vision, She is movement itself. She is the vibration of every note in every song, the shimmering liveliness of every atom. She is the waveform, the wave, the curve that disrupts the straight line. She is time itself (Kali) and keeps time through Her dance.

She is **attractive**. I use that word instead of the more common description of the feminine as "receptive," which sounds much too passive. She is magnetic. She directs by pulling you in, including you. She is a vortex. A seductress.

She is **sensual**. All human senses serve Her in lush harmonies of touch, sight, sound, taste, and scent. Her rituals feel luxurious, soft, and erotic. Relax and enjoy the sensations.

The Masculine

The Feminine created the masculine to serve a purpose. To be solid and supportive. To create perspective. To move from point A to point B with steady efficiency and elegance. Simple. Direct. Hardworking. Competent. Utilitarian. The masculine is the trellis that gives shape and support to Her growing vine. He is the scaffold She builds upon, and the stable form off which She may bounce, like light bounces off an object, to find new trajectories. Like any artist, She can find even greater variety of expression through limitation and containment. Just don't try to contain Her too long or too forcefully or She will break you. Use your strength to carry Her but don't try to hold Her down.

Masculinity adds a much-needed stability - the angles and straight lines that secure things, hold things up. The brute force to stand upright through gravity and lift Her ever higher.

Like a sculptor with rock or clay, She shapes the masculine into his most pleasing forms, and he thoroughly enjoys the feeling of being chiseled and molded. He is the firm ground through which Her roots can snake and grow, and his substance sustains Her.

The masculine is also a witness to Her endless creation, entranced and impassioned by Her movements, Her fluidity. She needs to be seen in order to know what She is. He can't stop marveling, sometimes perplexed, and often bewitched. He is made to frame Her and to use logic and mathematics as a means to describe Her creation and Her movement. He tries to catch the patterns and decipher the symbols and formulas in each vibration. His mode of understanding is comparison and categorization. But it's important to remember that really knowing Her is all about the experience and not about its description and interpretation.

The Perverse Masculine

It is as if long ago Devi brought forth the masculine and said, "Watch me, see me, describe me, take snapshots of my creation, give all my parts names, measure them, record them, interpret them, gather samples and arrange them in neat little boxes if you like, or set them on pedestals. I want to know what I am from all angles." His job was to be the feedback mechanism and the information storage device for all the data about everything She has done - all movement, matter, and creation. It allowed Her to repeat patterns and riff on themes; store codes in genes, replicable instructions in DNA.

And he was to build the temples in which She could be studied and worshiped. She asked him to behold Her and in so doing to hold Her and to venerate Her. That urge is still so strong in both the poet and scientist alike.

Things went wrong when he began to misinterpret the instructions. Instead of simply observing and recording, framing and showcasing, holding and supporting, he decided that She needed to be controlled and conquered. His descriptions turned into prescriptions. Instead of simply storing data for safekeeping, he fashioned a prison and then set out to capture and restrain the pieces of Her, nailing them into place like insects pinned to a board. Furthermore, he tried to harness the things he captured and put them to use for his own crude designs. Both inspired and envious, he wanted to be a creator, too. He fashioned his own god as masculine - the father - and tried to repress and forget the Mother from whence he came. Knowing Her, he began to think himself a master of Her. This is where the masculine lost his true purpose. He lost his way.

The Perverse Feminine

What happens when the feminine is held back, confined, dulled, stunted, or muted? What if you build a box or cage for Her that She cannot escape? That's when you get the Perverse Feminine. Frustration causes Her to be shaped into ugliness. She will seep into any crack or crevice and try to bust things open at the seams. The passive feminine is not calm. She's damned up and ready to blow. Passive aggression incarnate. If She has to, She will emulate the masculine to find freedom.

This is what we find within the patriarchal woman. She is artificially hardened. She will conquer and compete as a means of escape. And this is not just true of women, but men who try to actively repress the Feminine as well. They are often narcissistic and abusive.

The Dark Feminine

The Dark Feminine is not repressed and volatile like the Perverse Feminine. She dances in the shadows. She whispers secrets. She can be chaotic, unbound, unhinged. She is fierce compassion and spiritual ecstasy. If something is holding you back or standing in the way of heartfelt desire and creation, She will destroy it. And that can be absolutely terrifying. But in the end, it will leave you reborn and remade better off than before.

Intense, transformative experiences - non-ordinary states of mind, shaktipat (sudden realization), visions, and dreams are the forte of the Dark Feminine. We are currently in an era of the Dark Feminine emerging as things are shifting, and all that does not serve the best interests of the planet as a whole is being destroyed. If it's not collaborative it will not survive. This includes patriarchal social structures. Things buried in the collective unconscious will begin to surface for large numbers of people. We will remember things long forgotten. It may feel chaotic. It can be tumultuous but also ecstatic.

The image of the Goddess Kali or Inanna/Ishtar, Lilith, Hecate, and other Dark Goddesses are emblematic of the Dark Feminine. She is wild, mysterious, and a bit scary. But

Her purpose is to protect life (us included) as well as to create transformation and open up clogged paths of creation.

The Wild Feminine

If you have not seen the movie or read the book *Annihilation* written by Jeff Vandermeer, then you must. I would almost classify it as a Feminine religious text in disguise. Something happens to a place they call Area X. X points to the unexplainable, the mysterious, the unclassifiable. It becomes an otherworldly place where nature decides to stop making sense. Animals transform into plants and fungi. Everything is growing at an accelerated pace, in a constant state of change. Crystalline structures reach to the sky from the sand, and everything gets blended, every possible hybrid of life emerging and folding in on itself. Human consciousness is absorbed into the mix and algae write messages on dark tower walls. People who enter lose their grip on reason and analytical thought. They are annihilated via assimilation. Swallowed up in the psychedelic primordial freestyle biological jazz.

This is the perfect illustration of the Wild Feminine. It's the Feminine if She decided that the masculine was no longer needed and ate him. Unselfconscious, uncontained, ceaseless abundance, creation, and play. It is unsettling and even a little bit frightening. It's a place where surrender to the flow of rapid and constant evolution is the only option. There's nothing to hold onto. It's not necessarily a bad way to be, but the human mind would lose the ability to comprehend a thing.

Perhaps it is the fear of the Wild Feminine that gave

rise to the perverse masculine. The pervasive anxiety around the loss of definition and meaning drive him to aggressively grasp for control. It's the terror of annihilation. This wildness is why the masculine is important, just so long as he remembers where he came from and understands his purpose.

Ways of Knowing Her

All things to which we lend the descriptor of "feminine" or attribute to "femininity" will reflect the nature of the Feminine and Her qualities. Notice that weakness and passivity are not part of Her nature.

If you wish to know the Feminine, I will describe effective methods in my chapter on our new religion (a religion which is not entirely new but revived). In short, She wants you to be a unique channel for desire itself. Just keep in mind that you will know Her through experiential means, not analytical or intellectual means. You can't think or reason your way to Her, you must feel, sense, intuit. These are more direct and intimate, and less detached ways of knowing. You'll discover things you can't logically explain because logic is inherently quite limited. Some things *must* be described in the language of metaphor and symbols and poetic approximations. You will find them clearer and easier to understand that way. Thus is the nature of the Feminine.

| 2-4 |

Our Roles

One major purpose of giving importance to gender in the way we have is to delineate roles and shape the social structure. Roles help create cohesion and establish agreements. When in a group, knowing the role you play helps reduce social anxiety and also makes getting things done easier and more efficient. Having a variety of roles to fill makes a community strong and diverse.

Roles need not be rigid. We need not pick one role and stick with it. Roles can be contextual - dependent upon time, place, and company. They can also change as we change throughout our lives. We should always be wary of roles that become more prescriptive than practical. If ever it feels like you are putting on a role that doesn't feel authentic, switch it up!

To begin to establish the shape of Gynarchic society, I would like to suggest a non-exhaustive list of potential gendered roles and archetypes. It will help us imagine how our communities can be shaped. Use the list and see what resonates with you. In which roles do you see yourself? Which roles are you already occupying?

Roles for Women in Gynarchy

Roles for Women focus on their particular style of leadership or the unique power and strengths they bring to the Hive.

The Queenly Roles - These are the roles suited for the Women who are central leaders - the Queens of their Hives.

- **The Living Goddess** - She is the spiritual center of the Hive. Through Her own sadhana (spiritual practice), or through rites of consecration, She has become the literal and legitimate embodiment of the Divine Feminine. A real and true Goddess on earth. Men feel blessed that She accepts their worship and devotion. They build a Temple in which to be near Her. She is to be honored and revered, for She is sacred. She is both human and divine; She bridges the space between both worlds.

- **The Mother** - Whether she has actual children or not, the Mother is a nurturing presence in the lives of Her community. She leads with infinite compassion and is protective of her Hive family who always feel loved. She builds trust and authority with her patience and deep well of empathy. She instructs and guides with a firm but gentle hand.

- **The Visionary** - Her mind is lit up with new and future paradigms. From her vantage, she has an over-view of the big picture. She sees how all the pieces will come together. Her ideas and the way she conveys them inspire the Hive and make everyone want to move forward with all her plans. And she always has plans. She dreams impossible dreams and then scales them to the size of reality. She innovates her way forward fearlessly.
- **The Oracles** - These women only work in groups. Convening together their intuition is stronger and their power amplified. They are the decision-makers and the writers of laws. The congress and court rolled into one. They must be consulted on any important matter, and their wise consensus will guide the direction of everyone in the Hive.

Roles for Ladies of the Hive - including those who are not in the central role of Queen.

- **The Mistress** - The Mistress can be a classical Do-minatrix or simply a woman who is fond of taking control in a very direct and commanding way. When she speaks people listen and have the urge to obey. She is honest and direct about what she wants. She simply knows her power.
- **The Witch** - The Witch knows all about potions and plant medicine. You'll often find her convening with the elements as well as the ancestors. She is an expert

at setting intentions and implanting hypnotic sugges-
tions with her incantations. Nature loves a Witch, and
she wields its power with skill and care.

- **The Dakini** - Sometimes seen as a demoness, the
Dakini is an energy alchemist. She can turn fear into
ecstasy, pain into pleasure, weakness into resilience.
Known as sky dancers, Dakini have an ethereal quality
and their purpose is to lead their devotees toward a
higher understanding of themselves and the nature of
reality. Dakini are often gifted yoginis and tantrikas
and can be powerfully inspiring.

- **The Lady of Leisure** - She loves to be pampered
in every way, lavished with gifts, and surrounded by
luxury. Quality over quantity, of course. She is intelli-
gent and indulgent, and men love to indulge her. She's
all about sensuality and she may be involved in making
art or music or writing poetry or novels. Her ease
gives her time to ponder and imagine whole worlds
and develop finely honed aesthetics. She brings beauty
to everything.

- **The White Tigress** - The White Tigress seduces men
only to feed on their sexual energy and then dismiss
them. She can appear quite submissive at times in order to trigger men's lust - a carefully honed technique.
Her powerful sexual mojo keeps her and those around
her youthful and lively. She can drain a man dry and
leave him grateful for the experience. She may have
been a sex worker at some time in her life. No one
can own her, though many men crave her. She may

partner with a cuckold - a Jade Dragon who revels in her freedom.

- **The Teacher** - Her leadership style is instructive, and she loves to share information. Conversations with her are deep, philosophical, and intellectual. She is well-read and not shy about dishing out reading assignments or thought exercises. She may have an interest in psychology, physics, and history. She may be an expert in many things or focused on one specialty. Either way, knowledge is her power.

- **The Organizer** - Connecting people in a sense of community, and inspiring people to action are her superpowers. She's always thinking many steps ahead, her mind on the future, while taking inventory of the present and gleaning insightful lessons from the past. She knows where things belong, and the best times to act. She doesn't mind exerting effort and may enjoy planning elaborate parties, dinners, conferences, or anything where she can bring the skills, interests, and talents of others together in powerful ways.

- **The Separatist** - She wants little to nothing to do with men at all. She prefers the company of women and, if sexual, is only attracted to female bodies. She loves Gynarchy because of the sisterhood. The separatist isn't afraid to get her hands dirty as the idea of having men do things for her is distasteful. Her love for Women and her fierce independence are her greatest strengths.

- **The Housecat** - She doesn't seem all that dominant,

but everyone knows she rules the roost. She wants to be cuddled, petted, fed well, and cared for. Her personality is irresistibly adorable. She will likely allow men to care for her so long as they are not possessive, but she would be most loyal to a Woman. Like a cat, she is an enjoyable companion, playful and affectionate, but doesn't really allow herself to be controlled unless she wants to. She's sure to raise the serotonin and oxytocin levels of anyone who spends time with her.

Roles for Men in Gynarchy

Men's roles are mostly defined by their function - what they do within a community to serve and support the Women.

- **The Dasa** - the Dasa's entire life is about devotion to his Living Goddess. He is the ultimate Bhakta (devotee of the deity). He will play any other role necessary so long as it pleases his Goddess and makes Her life easier. His life is absorbed in the spiritual aspect of Gynarchy. He learns and enjoys the rites and rituals and understands their significance. Being knowledgeable in all aspects of Her worship, he can act as an emissary of the Living Goddess. For him, surrender and service are transcendent, and the very meaning of his existence.
- **The Knight** - The Knight is an honorable man, quite masculine, and with impeccable manners. He is proud to serve the Queen and will talk about it openly. He is romantic and chivalrous when it comes to Her, and

protective and loyal when it comes to the whole community. He never oversteps his bounds with a Lady; if he gives his word, you can rely on it. The Knight is most happy working as community security, never afraid to defend what he cares about, and he enjoys being a spokesman for the cause.

- **The Workhorse** - This man loves physical activity and will be happy sweating all day long to get a project done. He loves building things, digging holes, chopping wood, and putting his back into his labor. He's rugged and tough. When bored he lifts weights and hits the punching bag. He's a stallion and could take a beating if you need to spar. He gets restless without something to do that puts his strong body in motion.

- **The Handyman** - If something is broken, he knows how to fix it. He loves repairing things and keeping things maintained in good working order. Carpentry, plumbing, electrical, he's your go-to. He can build a shelf and probably fix your car, too. He loves his tools and knows the proper tool for every job. He is mechanically inclined and most proud of his problem-solving ability.

- **The Domestic** - The domestic finds great peace in making the home clean, tidy, and comfortable. He wants to make others feel at home. He knows all the ins and outs of doing laundry properly and can cook a delicious meal. He loves a neatly organized closet. His hospitality is unmatched. He's a bit of a perfectionist, but not in an annoying way, of course. Order in the house just makes him feel satisfied.

- **The Gardener** - The Gardener is a born nature lover. Give him a chance and all your produce will be home-grown and organic. You'll have more than you need and never go hungry. The trees and shrubs in your yard will also be healthy and well-pruned. He enjoys a well-maintained landscape. He knows about soil pH, beneficial insects, and much-needed microbes. He probably knows a bit about the medicinal uses of plants and could forage up something interesting if need be. He's the most sustainable man around.

- **The Caregiver** - If you are struggling, the caregiver is there to help take the load off. If you're sick or injured he will nurse you back to health. If you're hungry he will feed you. If you are mourning, he will be there to hold space or be a shoulder to cry on. He's a great listener. In good times he wants to pamper you and make you feel extra special. He is an expert at massage. He is also kind to children and makes an excellent and responsible babysitter. He pays attention to how his presence affects a Lady and always wants Her to feel nurtured and safe.

- **The Techie** - He knows what a coding marathon is. He can link up your intranet, build a website, and create a whole new currency without breaking a sweat. If you've got gadgets, he can show you how to make the best use of them. He can likely build computers from scratch. If he's bright, he can hack into systems he shouldn't and show you the security holes. He's your digital savant.

- **The Executive Assistant** - The EA knows everyone else's job and could hop in and take over in just about any role where he's needed. He will organize your day, thinking through every detail ten steps in advance. He anticipates your needs, even the ones you didn't know you had. He is aware of your favorite foods and dietary restrictions and will ensure lunch arrives on time. He's a researcher with encyclopedic knowledge; if he doesn't know, he will find out. And he's very adept at social situations, easing into any conversation with grace and intelligence and leaving a good impression.

- **The Renunciate** - He asks that you please do not praise him. He thrives on denial of pleasure coupled with tedious or repetitive work and topped off with flagellation. He'll do the dirty jobs no one else wants to do. He wants to feel insignificant. Just a robot, a cog in the machine of the community. Use him without reward and he feels right. He is most likely chaste. His spiritual disposition means he has a strict diet and denies himself any and all luxury. He is a stoic and a minimalist.

- **The Sexual Servant** - He has made it his lifelong study to learn how to please women sexually. He can do other things too, but giving sexual pleasure is his art form. His touch is ecstatic and connected. His oral skills are unmatched. He may sometimes play the service top to the Lady who needs to feel ravaged. He can also play the Jade Dragon to the White Tigress - a witness, cuckolded for Her pleasure, giving her tips on seduction, boosting Her confidence. Just seeing a woman cum excites him more than anything in the world, including his own orgasm.

- **The Patron** - His main contribution to any Queen or community is financial. He is great with money. He may have an important job out in the world, but he only does it to pour resources into the Woman or Women he serves. Because they deserve it. Giving gifts is how he shows his care and devotion. He expects nothing in return. Endlessly generous, he only feels valued when a Woman accepts his contributions. Being used for his money likely excites him.

- **The Pet** - He is Her emotional support animal. You may have heard of the "Golden Retriever Boy." That's him. He is completely loyal and always excited to be in Her presence. He is obedient to a fault and ever so affectionate. A real pleaser, with an extremely high emotional IQ. He can sense when she needs TLC. Such a good boy. He's great with kids and other animals. Treat him gently, give him lots of pets, and he will follow you anywhere.

- **The Gay Ally** - He has no sexual or romantic interest in women, but he absolutely loves to see us in power! His motto is something akin to "You go, girl!" He loves women and knows a woman-led world will be a better place. He shares our values. Some gay allies are a bit slutty and more than happy to offer their company to men who may need a sexual outlet when the women are not interested. They help to expand the sexual repertoire.

You may be wondering about more classical BDSM roles for men: sissies, masochists, fetishists. I see these as interests that could fit into the above roles. The gentle Domestic or the Caregiver might be a sissy, for example (Or just as likely not. It would be a mistake to assume that gentler men are feminized by default.), and any of the men might be masochistic or have various fetishes. The important thing is that the roles each man embodies feel authentic to him and bring fulfillment to both the Woman and himself.

I found that the problem men have had most in envisioning their place in a Hive was defining exactly what they had to offer to both Queen and community. When I ask, their sweet but useless answer is typically "Anything you want." So I made the men's roles about function, pushing men to envision what they will do and how they are useful. For some women the struggle was to understand how to wield power in their own way - thus the focus on women's unique powers and leadership styles.

Women's power coach Kasia Urbaniak often talks about the heavily gendered ways in which we are described when we are children. Boys are spoken about in reference to their actions ("Billy scored a goal." "Billy got into a fight."), and girls are described by their qualities ("Katie is so pretty." "Katie is sweet." "Katie is sassy."). I decided to both capitalize on this tendency by categorizing men by function and women by strengths and style, while at the same time subverting that habit by peppering descriptions of both actions and qualities throughout all of the roles.

You might wonder about an overarching structure around these roles or rules of conduct around how each relates to the other. If you have been paying attention to the concept of the Hive and the nature of the Feminine you will understand that every Hive is meant to operate according to the unique preferences of each Queen and the other women within the Hive. Relationship styles develop as they do in any free society, according to the needs and wants of the individuals involved. The Feminine loves variety, and norms and customs are developed organically through desire and consent. In the next section on Gynarchy-specific education, I will share some thoughts on family and relationships which might act as a guide to help further shape these norms in alignment with the principles of Gynarchy.

In imagining the roles, one can envision a colorful cast of characters that will make up our communities, interacting in different ways, all adhering to the Pillars of Gynarchy. More and more will evolve as each Hive is established. As an artist, I imagine creating trading cards, or better yet Tarot cards, with images, symbols, and meanings for all of the different roles, creating magical stories and readings from their combinations.

PART 3

GYNARCHY-ALIGNED EDUCATION

In some respects, understanding and implementing Gynarchy requires a bit of re-educating ourselves and unpacking the patriarchal biases that we've been taught since childhood. Our approach to History, Biology, Economics, Psychology, Religion, Relationships, and Sex will be understandably different. Our subjects will still be grounded in evidence, but we will emphasize different facets of each subject and take on different perspectives.

Education itself might be shaped a bit differently in Gynarchy. In an intellectually healthy society, all the topics I present here should simply be everyday topics of discussion. Kids should hear adults having deep conversations often (in age-appropriate ways) and be invited to join in, asking questions and adding their own insights. Basic literacy in subjects that shape the world and the human condition should be commonplace. Knowledge needs to be freely shared. And according to interest, each person will then take deeper dives into those areas that most fascinate them. Let their enthusiasm become contagious, inspiring others to learn more.

The approach to topics also needs to be relevant to how we live our lives. Mindless memorization should take a backseat to conceptual and nuanced understanding. All education should be participatory, and not handed down from on high. Expertise is still valued in Gynarchy, of course. Everyone knows something about something that you don't know. Even those people who tend to shy away from more obvious intellectual engagement have specialized knowledge and life experiences that can add to your understanding of the world.

What follows is a kind of syllabus and sampling of education under Gynarchy.

| 3-1 |

HISTORY

The history we've been taught is a history of conflict and war. As students, we're made to memorize the dates of battles and remember which nations ruled where and when. Wars are high-drama stories and, conveniently for historians, they usually have a clear beginning and end. Borders are emphasized and there is a tendency to highlight "great men," and concentrate on their individual contributions, even when most advances are in reality a group effort. "History is written by victors," is a quote attributed to Winston Churchill, and perfectly illustrates how we have traced our past under patriarchy.

History through a Gynarchic lens would emphasize great bursts of human creativity. We would cover the innovations of agriculture and the timeline of moving away from collaboration with the land and the subsequent return to that partnership. We'd talk about what we ate, how we made clothes and housing, how we managed water. Extraordinary discoveries, like germ theory and antibiotics, would still be included, and we'd examine how that impacted population, maternal and child mortality, and the like. We'd revel at how we've learned to use electricity and how electric light has changed our body's clocks and our sense of time. And we'd talk about how technology is used to ease the life of human-kind and improve our management of resources, and we'd understand the struggles along the way to be responsible in how we utilize it. We'd look at the innovation of steam and combustion engines, with a clear understanding of the nega-tive impacts of fossil fuels and the significance of new means of fulfilling our energy needs.

Social relationships and their different configurations across the world would be of particular interest to the Gynarchic historian. How did families, tribes, and societies organize themselves? We'd include the history of gendered power as I have included in this book, perusing the long list of examples of oppressive behaviors and policies. We'd look at the rise and fall of Patriarchy, including the victories and mistakes of feminism. We'd also examine the long-term effects of slavery and racism. We'd look at how governments came into being and the different forms they have taken, being sure to inventory their pros and cons. We'd look at successful methods and styles of conflict resolution through-out time. When there was resistance to power, why did it come about, and which kinds of resistance were most effec-tive and long-standing? (Spoiler: evidence shows that it was the non-violent kind.)

It would be vital to recognize groups and people who were oppressed and excluded but who nonetheless contributed much to their culture and to human life in general. Often the history of indigenous cultures is nearly forgotten, and it is essential that their stories not be lost. We must support the preservation of native languages and spiritual practices. We should have conversations with The Thirteen Indigenous Grandmothers comprised of elders from all over the world, and gain wisdom from their histories.

Most importantly we would remember women's contributions, which have often been ignored. From Hypatia to Émilie du Châtelet, we'd notice how women were able to find ways around their social status, and how society subsequently responded to them. Hypatia was murdered by the Christian church, for example, for gaining too much influence. Émilie du Châtelet dressed as a man to get into the intellectual salons and knew her pregnancy at age 39 was a death sentence.

We'd also examine how even feminism left out vast numbers of women in its early days of emancipation based on race, class, and ethnicity, and look at intersectionality. We'd read the poetry of Phillis Wheatly, who was kidnapped from West Africa and enslaved at age eight but went on to become the first African and Woman in the American colonies to publish a book. We'd study the 19th-century writings of African American suffragette Frances Ellen Watkins Harper.

We'd try to imagine a world where women were not oppressed and the kind of advancements that could have emerged. We'd also look at historical examples of Matriarchy across the planet, and how they compare to patriarchal cultures.

> *"While anthropologists question the existence of a true ma-triarchal society, there is a school of thought that believes that human society was originally matriarchal. During a period known as the 'Gynocratic Age,' women were allegedly worshiped for their ability to give birth. At this point, childbirth was a huge mystery, and men, not realiz-ing that they actually played a part in it, held the belief that women "bore fruit like trees when they were ripe." (We're talking about a really long time ago.) Allegedly, the Gynocratic Age lasted from around 2 million years ago to 3000 BCE."* (Natarajan)

We'd reach back into the Bronze Age to Minoan Crete, which most scholars agree was a thriving Matriarchy. We'd read the stories of Queen Arawelo, the Somali Queen who completely reversed the gender roles among her people in the 15th Century. We'd learn about Umoja, Kenya a commu-nity where men are forbidden, founded in 1990 by women who survived rape by British soldiers. We'd learn about the origins of the matrilineal Mosuo culture of China where marriage doesn't exist, and the Khasi tribe of India where only women own property. We'd study the history of the Minangkabau ethnic group of West Sumatra, Indonesia, the world's largest known matrilineal society where only women choose the political leaders.

We'd give special attention to the history of different arts, learning the history of music worldwide, as well as tex-tiles, literature, pottery, film, dance, sculpture, painting, and image-making of all kinds. Art museums would still be central education institutions, but they would be mindful never to steal from lands and people and only archive artifacts with the full acknowledgment and permission of the cultures from which they came. Cultural exchange replaces cultural appropriation. Archiving the full depth and breadth of human expression is a highly regarded occupation in Gynarchy.

Rosalind Miles' *Who Cooked the Last Supper: The Women's History of the World* would be required reading for the Gynarchist scholar who wants to know what women were doing while men were engaged in conquest and killing. Books like *A History of the World in Seven Cheap Things* by Raj Patel and Jason W. Moore would be included in a Gynarchic History curriculum. The authors look at how we've utilized, valued, and devalued nature, money, work, care, food, energy, and lives over time. In terms of the human condition, it's a much more informative take on history than recounting war strategies, rulers, and land grabs. We can't underestimate the way in which measuring history as a series of violent events is a self-perpetuating paradigm. Humans tend to try to imitate our heroes, measuring ourselves against the accomplishments of those who came before us. Wars may have changed languages and cultures significantly, but to use them as the metric by which we keep the time of civilization emphasizes a macho focus on conquest when there are so many other facets of our past to explore.

| 3-2 |

BIOLOGY

"[Darwinian] evolutionary biology is a more accurate re-
flection of pre-Victorian social practices than of natural
reality. In the wake of this metaphorical takeover, such
concepts as 'struggle for existence', 'competition', and 'fit-
ness' — which were central justifications of the political
status quo in (pre) Victorian England — tacitly became cen-
trepieces of our own self-understanding as embodied and
social beings. And they still are.... Biological, technological,
and social progress, so the argument goes, is brought forth
by the sum of individual egos striving to out-compete each
other. In perennial rivalry, fit species (powerful corporations) exploit niches (markets) and multiply their survival
rate (profit margins), whereas weaker (less efficient) ones
go extinct (bankrupt). This metaphysics of economics and
nature, however, is far more revealing about our society's

opinion about itself than it is an objective account of the biological world." (Weber)

Exploring the makeup of the natural world is a topic of never ending fascination for the Gynarchic scholar. There is a deep interest in the properties of plants, the functions of the body, and the reproduction and social organization of other species. Medicine in Gynarchy will lean heavily on the holistic understanding of human biology, how all systems work together, under the influence of both environment and behaviors.

As mentioned in a previous chapter, our creation myths can be closely linked to biology. It's common knowledge among biologists now that we all start out female in the womb. For the first six to seven weeks all fetal genitalia are the same and are phenotypically female. After that, if you have a Y chromosome with the SRY gene it will activate to inhibit certain features of the X chromosome and impose male physiological traits such as testicles. If the SRY is not activated, with or without the Y chromosome present, you remain female in phenotype and physical characteristics. The default body plan is basically female. One can reproduce with just one X chromosome unless that SRY gene on the Y chromosome flips the switch and renders you unable to birth new life.

In *Women After All: Sex, Evolution, and the End of Male Supremacy*, behavioral biologist and anthropologist Dr. Melvin Konner points to evidence that our distant ancestors also started out as all female with the capability of parthenogenesis. We could reproduce without the need for sexual fertilization.

"There is a birth defect that is surprisingly common, due to a change in a key pair of chromosomes. In the normal condition the two look the same, but in this disorder one is shrunken beyond recognition. The result is shortened life span, higher mortality at all ages, an inability to reproduce, premature hair loss, and brain defects variously resulting in attention deficit, hyperactivity, conduct disorder, hypersexuality, and an enormous excess of both outward and self-directed aggression. The main physiological mechanism is androgen poisoning, although there may be others. I call it the X-chromosome deficiency syndrome, and a stunning 49 percent of the human species is affected. It is also called maleness.

My choice to call being male a syndrome and to consider it less normal than the usual alternative is not (as I will show you) an arbitrary moral judgment. It is based on evolution, physiology, development, and susceptibility to disease. Once in our distant past, all of our ancestors could reproduce from their own bodies; in other words, we were all basically female. When biologists ask why sex evolved, they are not asking rhetorically—the fact that sex feels good was a valuable addition. What they are really asking is: Why did those self-sufficient females invent males? It had to be a very big reason, since they were bringing in a whole new cast of characters that took up space and ate their fill, not to mention being quite annoying, but could not themselves realize the goal of evolution: creating new life."

Dr. Konner expounds upon the many configurations of sex among species in the animal kingdom, some of which have even phased out the male sex because the cost of supporting maleness outweighs its evolutionary advantages. And his answer to the question of why the male sex entered the equation in the first place comes down to what's called "the Red Queen hypothesis." It's named after the character in Alice's Wonderland, and the line "It takes all the running you can do to keep in the same place." In evolutionary terms, "It takes all the evolving you can do to keep in the same place." Our environment keeps changing, and as we evolve the things that can kill us also evolve to catch up. This is especially true for the predators that destroy us from within: parasites, viruses, and germs. Antibiotic-resistant bacteria is one good example. To stay alive we need a lot of excess DNA, lots of variations to make their job harder. We have to keep changing things up. If we simply clone ourselves, reproducing without sex, these invasive predators only have to figure out how to get at us once. Ultimately immunity depends on genes. It's a game of chess between us and the microbes. In short, males evolved to provide a greater variety of genes. They simply store and pass on genetic information that we can mix and match in endless variations over generations, making our species hardier and more disease resistant.

What irony, however, that in creating the male sex to protect ourselves from tiny invasive predators, we also created what turns out to be one of the female human's biggest external predators: men. Is it any wonder the black widow spider eats her mate?

There is some evidence that the Y chromosome in humans is being phased out. It has gradually carried fewer and fewer genes and is growing smaller over time.

> *"Y chromosomes have a fundamental flaw. Unlike all other chromosomes, which we have two copies of in each of our cells, Y chromosomes are only ever present as a single copy, passed from fathers to their sons.*
>
> *This means that genes on the Y chromosome cannot undergo genetic recombination, the "shuffling" of genes that occurs in each generation which helps to eliminate damaging gene mutations. Deprived of the benefits of recombination, Y chromosomal genes degenerate over time and are eventually lost from the genome."* (Griffin, Ellis)

This process of discontinuation will likely take millions of years, however. And meanwhile, if we survive all that time, evolution will figure out a way for us to reproduce in other ways. Perhaps through a modified version of sexual reproduction, or maybe returning us back to our parthenogenetic roots.

Nicolas Hartsoeker's illustration of a tiny proto-person inside a sperm cell, 1694

Patriarchal understanding of biology started out on shaky ground. I am not joking when I say that male doctors used to hypothesize that a man's sperm contained a whole tiny little baby that he plants like a seed in a woman's womb to grow. We still use the word "seed" to refer to sperm as a result. The biologists of hundreds of years ago, making guesses without the benefit of high powered microscopes, were not the only ones to come up with faulty assumptions. In the past fifty years, we've discovered that the woman's body and the ovum play an active role in getting the sperm to their destination. Those spiraling tails help with motility, but it's not the heroic race to the finish portrayed in popular culture. It turns out even dead sperm can get moved through the fallopian tubes.

> *"For instance, most mammalian sperm do not in fact swim up the entire female tract but are passively transported part or most of the way by pumping and wafting motions of the womb and oviducts... Convincing evidence has instead revealed that human sperm are passively transported over considerable distances... So much for Olympic-style racing sperm!"* (Martin)

And, it also turns out, the ovum is surrounded by follicular fluid which contains chemicals called chemoattractants. The egg chooses sperm through attraction (the Feminine is attractive).

> "Human eggs use chemical signals to attract sperm. New research from Stockholm University, Manchester University NHS Foundation Trust and The University of Manchester shows that eggs use these chemical signals to "choose" sperm. Different women's eggs attract different men's sperm – and not necessarily their partners." (University of Manchester)

Furthermore, that old notion that men's fertility far outlasts women's has also been revealed to be another macho myth.

> "Another dangerous misconception is the myth that men retain full fertility into old age, starkly contrasting with the abrupt cessation of fertility seen in women at menopause. Abundant evidence shows that, in men, sperm numbers and quality decline with increasing age. Moreover, it has recently emerged that mutations accumulate about four times faster in sperm than in eggs, so semen from old men is actually risk-laden." (Martin)

Early patriarchal biologists came up with ideas like "wandering wombs," wherein the organ drifts all over inside the body, affecting other organs. They concluded that this was due to a woman having not gotten pregnant at a young age. It took a long time for them to figure out that the clitoris existed and that its sole purpose is to give a woman pleasure. The idea that women had orgasms was quite novel (which speaks volumes concerning men's skill as sexual partners). And how strange that, though the female body is the default model, women's bodies have been left out of medical research in ways that have had detrimental effects on our health. Adding insult to injury, women's symptoms are also often ignored by doctors for much longer periods of time than those of men.

Biology is an important subject to understand in order to understand Gynarchy, an ideology that is enmeshed in concepts of sex and gender. But more than that, understanding how all living systems on this planet work helps us to be responsible stewards of the land and work in harmony with nature in all areas of life. A deeper understanding of the soil and plant life, and the interrelated nature of all species in a given biome, make sustainable farming possible, providing abundance for generations to come. Understanding how various chemicals affect air and water quality and alter our bodies helps keep all living things healthy and prevents many diseases. Climate science may help us stave off extinction and the decimation of resources. An earnest study of plant medicine can be lifesaving. Biology is not just an interesting area of study, it's knowledge that is essential to our survival.

"The evolutionary biologist and futurist Elisabet Sathouris describes how in the evolution of complex communities of diverse organisms a 'maturation point' is reached when the system realizes that "it is cheaper to feed your 'enemies' than

to kill them." Having successfully populated six continents and diversified into the mosaic of value systems, world-views, identities (national, cultural, ethnic, professional, political, etc.) and ways of living that make up humanity, we are now challenged to integrate this precious diversity into a globally and locally collaborative civilization acting wisely to create conditions conducive to life." (Wahl)

Just as the pre-Victorian interpretation of Darwin's "survival of the fittest" reflected how society felt about itself and was used to justify competition and exploitation, this newer systems-based view of biology and evolution reflects the collaborative thinking and attitudes of Gynarchy as a worldview.

| 3-3 |

ECONOMICS

"Nietzsche's madman announcing the death of god was met in a similar fashion.... The twenty-first century has an analogue: it's easier for most people to imagine the end of the planet than to imagine the end of capitalism." (Patel)

Economics has taken on the feel of team sports. Work-a-day passive participants in the game still passionately root for their favorite "ism." Capitalism, socialism, libertarianism. No one can talk publicly about economic ideas without being accused of being either a heartless capitalist or a dirty commie when in truth very few people are either. Unless you are a wealthy business owner, you're just a consumer, not a capitalist, and even the most ardent proponent of communism is still beholden to the laws of the state where he lives.

The divisive discourse may persist because the field itself is dominated by men. In 2022, depending on the country, only between 18 and 30% of economists were women. This has a pronounced effect on our style of engagement around economic issues. This macho war of isms is not particularly useful and only serves to stifle imagination regarding what's possible and what best supports life on the planet. No other topic highlights what people choose to value like the discussion of economics. And more than anything, it illustrates to what degree we value our fellow humans.

Do you believe that a person, by virtue of being born here on Earth, is automatically entitled to their basic necessities like food, clean water, and shelter? Or do you believe we all need to learn to fend for ourselves, to work hard to meet our own needs or perish, and that no one owes us a living? Your particular take on economics is going to be almost entirely dictated by how you answer. Which approach do you think most aligns with the ideology of Gynarchy?

> *"If we want to re-design economics based on what we know about life's strategy to create conditions conducive to life, we need to question some basic assumptions upon which the narrative underlying our current economic systems is built. The narrative of separation has predisposed us to focus on scarcity, competition, and the short-term maximization of individual benefit as the basis on which to create an economic system. Life's evolutionary story shows that systemic abundance can be unlocked through collaboratively structured symbiotic networks that optimize the whole system so human communities and the rest of life can thrive."* (Wahl)

It's helpful to ask the women who take an interest in economics and business what they think; in Gynarchy, their voices are incredibly important. Jennifer Armbrust holds a degree in Critical Theory and Political Economy with advanced studies in small business administration, and she created an organization called Sister, where she coaches others on entrepreneurship grounded in feminine principles. Typically, feminist economics draws attention to things like the value of women's unpaid labor in the home. Feminine economics is a different approach to how we do business. The goal is still to make money as we create value, but Armbrust espouses an underlying set of ethics and a mindset that seeks to prioritize connection and positions quality of life over profits. She wants to create a new business archetype. Some words she uses to describe a Feminine Economy are abundance consciousness, generosity, interdependence, ease, collaboration, embodiment, cyclical growth, honesty, and sustainability. Her twelve principles include "institutionalize empathy," and "consider everything an experiment." She refers to her approach as "Capitalist-critical."

> *"This is about redistributing power and resources. This is about radical social transformation. A feminist business can model new ways of living, working, and being together. This is about transforming our relationship to money,to work, to the Earth, to our bodies, and to each other. "*

> *"You hear 'the divine feminine' a lot, but we don't know exactly what that means. All of a sudden it has something*

to do with buying yoga clothes, maybe. Stealing words back from advertising and understanding their meaning and their historical context is crucial. That education piece is a big part of what I'm doing; it's why my work involves the school and teaching, not just consulting." (Zurer)

On the more radically gyn-anarchist end of the spectrum are ideas like gift economies. In a gift economy, the goal is not to make money off the value you create but to create a thriving, happy, caring community wherein everyone gets their needs met. It works well for smaller communities where everyone has a skill or craft to contribute. You garden, cook meals, make clothes and other goods, build things, clean up, babysit, heal people, repair things, teach skills and you gift your goods and services to whoever needs or wants them with no expectation of anything in return. You aren't bartering, you're just taking care of your people. Gift economies can also be a place where the excesses of consumerism can be put to good use, with free stores giving out used and upcycled goods and lending out tools, equipment, and other large items from large communal lending libraries.

"The gift economy is not a novel concept. Its first studies came from anthropologists Bronislaw Malionwski and Marcel Mauss who recorded the "imponderabilia of everyday life" in the Trobriand Islands. There, tribesmen living on the islands took dangerous canoe journeys across miles of ocean to participate in the kula, a ceremonial exchange of shell necklaces and arm bracelets. These items were

received as friendship tokens and carried with them an obligation to continue the exchange. Through circling these ceremonial mementos, tribesmen were able to gain social credit and cement bonds between families and clans.

Compared to the market economy in which people build a relationship based on the items traded, the gift economy focuses on building a relationship between the people trading. In fact, repaying a gift, immediately or with something of exactly equal value, may be read as ending the social relationship. Rather than accumulating material wealth, participants in a gift economy grow richer through obtaining social capital. The affluent give away what they don't need to increase their status. As people take care of other members in their community, the community will take care of them." (Peng)

It's reasonable to think that a Hive within Gynarchy could easily implement a gift economy as the emphasis is on creating small-scale communities within a larger network. Gift economies do tend to fail on a larger scale because of freeloaders and mistrust. The key to a thriving gift economy is close connection and intimacy within the community and a code of ethics that everyone agrees on with enthusiasm. In such communities, gift economies are a way to create bonds and spread trust and goodwill. A Hive is only as valuable as the work, skills, and talents of all its members combined. All hives will survive, and some Hives will be absolutely wealthy with resources. In such cases, their abundance could spill over into the network and the other communities around them.

Think of the old bedtime story of *Stone Soup*. A traveler arrives at a hungry village with nothing but a pot. He begins to cook with only water from the well and a stone he finds on the ground, and the curious and hungry villagers ask what he's making. He tells them it's stone soup. "Impossible!" They say, "You can't make soup from a stone!" He says the stone is magical. He tells them each, one by one, that the soup is just about ready, but it would be better with just one more ingredient. And one by one they each add an ingredient to the soup: herbs, butter, vegetables, chicken. In the end, he's made a marvelous stew which he shares with everyone, and no one goes hungry.

Despite my problems with the Abrahamic religions, I have to give Islam credit for making one of its pillars Zakat - a law wherein every Muslim must give a percentage of their income to community members in need. And when I traveled to the Middle East, I noticed a charming habit of Iraqi Arabs. If you compliment them on some item they own, they will offer it to you. "Take it," they say, warding off envy. And you have to refuse three times or it will be given to you. Charity and generosity are lovely, but I often think they don't go far enough. Building all of society on principles of abundance and connectedness is a much-needed remedy to the income disparity and greed of our current systems.

Because of the horizontal structure of Gynarchy, I tend not to talk about economies that rely on the state or other top-down authority to distribute value. However, in reality, a

Hive might agree to pool their money and resources in such a way that the Queen or Queens can use and distribute them in whatever way is most beneficial to the Hive. Members might create businesses together and share their resulting income and expenses in a collective account, controlled by the Queen. They might work outside the Hive and do the same. This requires great trust, but this kind of trust is built between business partners all the time. There is a higher chance of hoarding and greed in such an arrangement. However, the safeguard is the consensual nature of Gynarchy itself. If the person in charge abuses you, financially or otherwise, you simply leave and take your resources with you. If enough people leave the group is diminished and weakened.

Madeline Pendleton is an incredible business innovator who lives by the economic values of Gynarchy. She started out broke and intermittently homeless. She is now the sole owner and CEO (Queen?) of her multi-million-dollar clothing brand Tunnel Vision. She and all her employees make the exact same take-home pay, have full benefits, and take unlimited paid time off. All profits are distributed equally between the employees and don't just go back into her pocket. Her business has been around for over 11 years and is doing well. It turns out that when employees have a lot to gain from a company's success, they work hard to make it successful.

Madeline says, "I've done a lot of stuff that people told me was impossible to do… and I didn't do it in, like, a 'pull yourself up by your bootstraps, the economy is fine,' way. I did in a kicking, screaming, clawing, 'the economy is killing us and I refuse to go down without a fight,' way." Her book about how she did it is called *I Survived Capitalism and All I Got Was This Lousy T-Shirt.*

All economies are collaborative by necessity. However, in Gynarchy, the most crucial goal is to ensure the collaborators are not exploited to funnel resources to a few. This might be as simple as using co-op models for any businesses created, where every worker has a stake in ownership and takes a share of the surplus income.

Another advantage of the Hives and Network model of Gynarchy is that every Hive's economy could be completely different from that of the next. And as the Queens connect with other Queens from different Hives they discuss and share everything about how their Hive runs. In this way, both economic and social models can be refined and perfected through the amassed wisdom of the network. Knowledge is free and open source.

Sustainability and interdependence are valued over profits. The profit motive is the enemy of true abundance. This is a principle that must be taught in Gynarchic economics. We make good use of social capital and operate from a sharing mindset, not fear of lack. And as with the honeybee, no bee will starve unless the Hive starves. Think of the deficit of empathy and the amount of survival anxiety and fear it takes to allow another person to suffer without their basic human needs. These are not things the Gynarchy can tolerate.

| 3-4 |

PSYCHOLOGY

Psychology interrogates the causes and effects of our behaviors, thoughts and feelings, which erupt from a symphony of factors. Our family dynamics, social relationships, survival stress, traumas, culture, biology, gender, gut microbiome, and, as I mentioned in a previous chapter, our epigenetics and the collective unconscious all play a part in shaping our psyches. It's a complex area of study, and a kind of an art and a science rolled into one.

In an actual conversation with my child, I mentioned that men, in general, tend to be a bit messier than women.

"Mom!" they objected haughtily, "That's so sexist!"

"Have you ever seen men's public restrooms?" I responded.

Just because something may sound sexist doesn't make it untrue. The fact is there are some general trends in tendencies and behaviors that can be observed as belonging to one gender or another. Have I met extremely messy women? Yes! I even dated one. Have I known men who are neat and tidy?

You bet. But as a group, there's a tendency for women to care more about cleanliness.

Some gendered statements have been shown to be demonstrably false. We used to think that, among our earliest ancestors, men hunted and women gathered as a general rule. But archaeological evidence shows that women hunted about as often as men, and they did so in packs, whereas men often liked to hunt alone or with one other man. "Women can't hunt," is shown as false, so persisting with that stereotype is just an unsupported bias. And that's truly sexist.

I also had to explain to my child the role of power dynamics in sexism, and the concepts of punching up or punching down. Even if a statement is hurtful or false, if it is said about a group that has more power, it doesn't have the same impact as when the insult or snipe is aimed at a group that has very little power. Just as "Cracker" and the N-word don't pack anywhere near the same punch. It may sting a bit on an individual basis, but it's not like any public policies will be enacted as a result of a biased statement against the group in power. And if one feels personally hurt by a truthful generalization, it might be time to take a look at that truth and figure out why the pattern exists. Or you could simply realize that the statement doesn't apply to you, even if it applies to many people of your gender.

In any science, one looks for repeatable patterns and builds theories around them. If you are researching swans, for example, and all you ever see are white swans, you can surmise that swans are generally white. If one black swan comes along, you can still say that swans are generally white, with some exceptions. The more data you have, the better your generalizations. It may turn out that worldwide, half of all swans are pink, but until you observe that, it is safer to stick with the original generalization.

Gender Psychology

The psychological makeup and behaviors of men and women show some marked differences on average. To deny that in the name of equality is to support a lie to fit an agenda. It is good to examine statements for validity, however, especially across cultures and over time. It may be that women in Country A and Country B exhibit very different behaviors in some regards but share the same behaviors and tendencies in others. The same is true when observing women now as opposed to women 50 or 100 years ago. And it could be that changing the way in which you collect the data, such as asking slightly different questions, will change your results. As always, the more observations and data you collect, the more accurate your generalizations will be. As I said, the field of psychology and human behavior is a bit of an intuitive art as well as a science.

So why might we want to know about the psychological differences between men and women in the first place? The first reason is to help with communication. Understanding each other's underlying motives and feelings can help prevent misunderstandings. Secondly, it can help determine what our strengths and weaknesses are as a group, and what social roles we are best suited for. As fun as it may sound, we might want to avoid putting a woman-shaped peg into a man-shaped hole (insert giggles). Finally, remaining open to inevitable exceptions helps to prevent this knowledge from being weaponized.

The Gynarchist psychologist, of course, takes a particular interest in the gendered differences in behaviors, thinking, and feeling. And we're not alone. We have a lot of previous research to help inform our studies. The American Psychological Association's PsycINFO database (http://psyc-net.apa.org) includes 89,415 journal articles published from 1950 through 2021 that focus on these comparisons, with over 700 meta-analyses of previous studies. I think it's fair to say most of us can already intuitively sense generalized gender differences among our fellow humans. That's why psychologists have done so much research on the topic in the first place. If I gave you a list of behaviors and psychological characteristics, you could accurately guess the gender of the person described, without having seen a photo or met them, 85% of the time (that was part of a real study called *Global sex differences in personality: Replication with an open online dataset*). To be scientific, we just need to verify how accurate our intuition may be as objectively as possible.

And before I move forward, I want to make it clear that this information should not be used to dehumanize any gender. We may be very different in some ways, but we are all unique humans. Connections rather than divisions are always preferred in Gynarchy. And this knowledge of gendered differences should be able to help us find our happy place - our best and most fulfilling roles within our communities. They should also lend us a better understanding of, and facilitate better relationships between, opposite genders.

Autism has been called "extreme male brain." There's a reason for that.

> "In the mid-1990s, British researcher Simon Baron-Cohen incorporated tests of social intelligence and pattern recognition into his autism studies. In the general population, these tests show sex differences: Women tend to perform well on the tests of social intelligence, whereas men tend to excel at following rules and recognizing patterns. Baron-Cohen found that autistic people generally have trouble with the former but do well with the latter.
>
> In 2002, he proposed the extreme male brain theory of autism to account for these findings. He and his colleagues then developed a pair of self-report questionnaires to measure systemizing abilities.
>
> Baron-Cohen's team analyzed responses to these questionnaires from 600,000 people, including 36,874 with autism. The results suggest that autistic men and women both tend toward systemizing.
>
> Baron-Cohen's other work hints at where this tendency may originate. Some people with autism may have been exposed to elevated levels of sex steroid hormones, such as testosterone, in utero, he says. Excess testosterone may alter the structure of the developing brain in ways that affect thinking patterns." (Furfaro)

This data is echoed by other studies that show that, on average, women have a tendency to be more socially collaborative and empathetic.

For example, a 2010 study by organizational psychologist Anita Williams Woolley, PhD showed that groups with a higher number of women showed more "collective intelligence" which means the ability to work together to solve a wide range of problems. And they made better use of the knowledge of everyone in the group by displaying better conversational turn-taking. And studies like *Gender and leadership style: A meta-analysis* by Eagly in 1990, show that women tend more toward a democratic and collaborative leadership style. A large study in 2022 at the University of Cambridge showed that women tend to possess more cognitive empathy - the ability to understand what others are thinking and feeling.

> *"In 36 countries, women scored on average significantly higher in their cognitive empathy scores than men did. In 21 of the countries, women's and men's scores were similar. There wasn't a single country in which men scored better, on average, than women. The results held across eight languages and were consistent across the lifespan, from people ages 16 to 70 years old."* (Christensen)

These are prosocial advantages that make women better at leading and guiding others without force and with less conflict. In fact, in many surveys in the workplace, employees report feeling more motivated to work when supervised by a female boss than a male boss. This is despite previous outdated notions that showing too much compassion makes one an ineffective leader.

> "Women may exhibit more intuition, empathy, collaboration, self-control, and appropriate concern because of increased blood flow in the brain. Or as Dr. Daniel Amen, Founder of the Amen Clinics, put it: 'The female brain is wired for leadership.'
>
> Research on nonverbal communication skills shows women are better at reading facial expressions and emotions. As a result, we are more likely to pick up on the subconscious cues of others. The University of Cambridge conducted an experiment by showing people pictures of eyes. The subjects were then asked to conclude the person's mood based on the appearance of the eyes in the photo. Unsurprisingly, the ladies dominated.
>
> When comparing MRI scans of brain activity, the female brain reveals an increased number of neural connections. This makes it more efficient and helps with interpreting one's social surroundings."

Despite being more empathetic and intuitive, research has disproved the assumption that women are "more emotional" than men, however. We're generally pretty close to the same in regard to our *internal experience* of emotions. The way we express emotion is often quite different. Women cry more, but men, on average, display more volatile emotions like anger. Covering up their feelings with displaced anger is a defense mechanism more common to men. And some research indicates that men suffer more stress from repressing their more vulnerable emotions.

How do gender differences show up in regard to mental health? Male suicide rates are climbing, and men are about four times more likely to successfully commit suicide. But in contrast to those statistics, women are about three times more likely to be clinically depressed than men, and two to four times more likely to attempt suicide without success. And women are twice as likely to suffer from anxiety disorders. These numbers could be slightly skewed because women get help more readily for mental health problems, but it also could be partly because women still struggle to have real safety and autonomy in a male-dominated society.

If women are cut out for compassionate leadership, what are men's inherent strengths, and how are they unlocked? The Gynarchal Psychologist might be interested to know the kinds of emotional experiences that tap into their natural inclinations. The consensus among surveys is that men want to feel needed and useful. Most enjoy praise and want to feel competent. "Praise training," as women's power coach Kasia Urbaniak calls it, can work with anyone, but it is especially effective with men.

They like to be given direct instructions, and not have to guess what someone needs. But men are also great at pattern recognition, so if you do something the same way or at the same time every day, he will catch on quickly and anticipate it. Rituals and routines can put his mind at ease.

Men generally like a sense of purpose. They want their

life to mean something. A man who doesn't feel he's working toward something important can become disheartened. Very masculine men, especially, need to be given a goal or a project to prevent them from becoming listless. Ask a man for help or to solve a problem, and he will feel a sense of pride in being of assistance. It is my observation that men quite love being used well, and even being given challenges that allow them to show off what they are capable of. From their own self-reported list of psychological needs and tendencies, it's easy to see how the evolved man would find incredible satisfaction in Gynarchy as he serves his Queen and Hive. Doing so checks all the boxes in terms of bolstering masculine happiness.

Developmental Psychology

Gender psychology is not the only area with which we should concern ourselves, however. Developmental psychology will help us raise future generations in a healthy way in alignment with our values. The Gynarchist knows that the pillars of Consent and Bodily Autonomy are not just important among adults. We recognize the mounds of research that overwhelmingly shows that authoritarian styles of parenting, such as spanking and punishment, are less effective and more harmful than gentle, cooperative parenting. Clear and logical boundaries and the freedom to discover who they are is what kids need. Our goal as parents is to teach and guide, not force kids into conformity. Like women, children have been oppressed and abused under strict patriarchal childrearing standards. The Gynarchist recognizes that spanking is an inherently sexual activity, which releases tension and ramps up endorphins, and is not to be engaged in with children. And it has a strong correlation with substance abuse later in life. So always spare the rod. The child will grow up with fewer mental health issues that way.

Group Dynamics

And since developing small communities and a vast network are the goals of Gynarchy, it is helpful to study group dynamics. What helps bring people together and create a genuine sense of belonging? Through the study of social psychology, we know that a few of those things include shared values, shared symbols, shared stories, and shared rituals.

We also know which toxic group dynamics may be very attractive at first, but inevitably devolve into abusive games of control designed to feed the ego of a singular figurehead. One of those is the way in which a damaging cult will create separation between a member of the group and their loved ones outside the group. The psychological mechanisms behind this "us or them" mentality are indistinguishable from those of nationalism or racism. Being accepted into a very insular and exclusive "in group" makes one feel special. However, when exposed to outside logic, the indoctrination can often fall apart and leave one feeling lost and disoriented. This is true of some sects of Christianity as well as corporate-style cults like NXIVM. Upon leaving these groups, individuals might struggle to regain an authentic sense of self. Since Gynarchy puts a high value on autonomy and authenticity, it is important for us to look out for these pitfalls and dysfunctional relationships and avoid them.

Non-Ordinary States of Consciousness

There is a branch of psychology that looks at the unconscious and the phenomena of states of mind which are outside the norms of mundane existence. Things like religious ecstasy, visions, lucid dreams, or the use of psychedelic plants bring on transient states which often have a deep impact on the mind and the life of the person undergoing such a journey.

> *"Several studies have recently suggested that the therapeutic value of psychedelic experiences may lie in their ability to increase or facilitate mental flexibility, insight, and acceptance (Carhart-Harris & Friston, 2019). One of the leaders in the field of psychedelic research, Robin Carhart-Harris, has proposed an entropic theory of consciousness to help explain and understand how this process might work (2018). Essentially, this theory suggests that many or most mental health concerns are associated with a reduced level of psychological and cognitive flexibility. In essence, the brain/mind becomes stuck in certain patterns that are no longer useful to the person. By introducing a powerful experience that shifts awareness into a broader perspective and expression, it is possible to help the mind become "unstuck." When this process is conducted in a therapeutic context with ongoing therapy, it can potentially enhance outcomes."* (Terrant)

These experiences are the native language of the Dark

Feminine, and so are of great interest to the Gynarchist. Psychiatrists like Carl Jung and Christina and Stanislav Grof have cataloged these extraordinary occurrences and have found many common symbols and motifs which run as connecting threads through humans of all different backgrounds and identities. To the Gynarchist, these are like a download of knowledge from Devi Herself which helps us gain new perspectives. They open us to old collective wisdom that has sometimes been forbidden or hidden.

The understanding of how to create non-ordinary states should be used to create powerful rituals, as well as provide healing and insight to individuals of the Hive. Living Goddesses use these states as a regular part of their religious practice through meditation and trance. So understanding their significance is important to understanding the religious practices of Gynarchy.

...

So many fields of psychology are useful and interesting within the context of Gynarchy, and they serve to help us contextualize our ideology and better understand one another.

| 3 - 5 |

WORLD RELIGIONS

"They come to ask for her teachings.

They say, "Why do you call God 'She'?"

Eve says, "God is neither woman nor man but both these things. But now She has come to show us a new side to Her face, one we have ignored for too long."

They say, "But what about Jesus?"

Eve says, "Jesus is the son. But the son comes from the mother. Consider this: which is greater, God or the world?"

They say, for they have learned this already from the nuns, "God is greater, because God created the world."

Eve says, "So the one who creates is greater than the thing created?"

They say, "It must be so."

Then Eve says, "So which must be greater, the Mother or the Son?"

— Naomi Alderman, *The Power*

The Abrahamics

In an uncharacteristically frank account of religious history, an American Messianic Jewish rabbi by the name of Jonathan Cahn appeared on religious talk shows to explain to groups of fundamentalist Christians about the signs of the return of the Goddess, Inanna - The Enchantress. And just about everything he said rang true. People have turned away from the god of Abraham, and huge transformations are taking place.

Cahn was promoting his New York Times bestseller called *The Return of the Gods*. He wrote it as a warning rather than a celebration, but it is essentially grounded in fact. He writes about the old gods of the Middle East - of ancient Canaan and Phoenicia - being exiled, driven underground, so to speak, by the followers of his own god, Yahweh. He gives biblical references, providing no recourse for the Christian in denial of the ancient gods' existence. And he tells the reader, though they were once beloved and revered, these gods are bad, and, after they were driven out, his god replaced them in the hearts of humans. It turns out, Cahn says, they have re-surfaced again, coming out of exile, and are slowly regaining their place in the modern world. Evidence of this is found in the sexual revolution of the 1960s, the fight for abortion rights, as well as the Stonewall Riot, and contemporary trans rights activism.

The story he tells is the story of a sort of cleansing in the ancient world to make way for the laws of his own deity - a deity who makes claims about his sole role in creation (sound familiar?). This god's followers were guided to reject and forget the Divine Feminine, to deny the Mother. The followers even demoted their own god's wife, the once beloved Asherah, to a demoness, and then attempted to write her out of the picture entirely. We know from archaeological evidence that the ancient Israelite religion was polytheistic until about the 7th century BCE or even later, with a whole pantheon of different gods and goddesses. Yahweh absorbed all of their attributes in a concerted effort to make the holy father the one and only head of the household.

Likewise, one of the first things Muhammad did to establish Islam in Mecca was to walk into the Kaaba, which had been a pagan temple built around a vulva-shaped meteorite and destroy all of the idols of the Arabian Goddesses Manat, Lat, and Uzza within it. Early on there was a verse accepted as part of the revealed Quran affirming the worship of this Feminine trinity, but then Muhammad had another revelation and a change of heart, and he wrecked the place. In order for a masculine godhead to take a firm hold, he had to eliminate the Feminine. These are the so-called "Satanic Verses."

"Near it is the Garden of Abode. Behold, the Lote-tree was shrouded (in mystery unspeakable!) (His) sight never swerved, nor did it go wrong! For truly did he see, of the Signs of his Lord, the Greatest! Have ye seen Lat. and 'Uzza, And another, the third (goddess), Manat?

These are the exalted cranes (intermediaries) Whose intercession is to be hoped for."

Man kissing the black stone (hajarulaswad) set into the Eastern corner of the Kaaba in Mecca. According to Muslim tradition it dates back to the time of Adam and Eve.

When I traveled to Iraq, I had the opportunity to sit down with one of the country's most prominent Islamic scholars. The borders had just opened to foreigners after ousting Saddam Hussein, and he was eager to speak about the West after such a long period of isolation. He was fascinated to learn about the new and neo-pagan religions being practiced in the United States. He took notes as I explained Scientology, and as I listed off different pagan groups, from Wiccans to

Dianics. When I told him there were some who worshiped Inanna, his eyes lit up. "Ah!" he exclaimed with a grin, "Our Mother!" Anyone who studies Abrahamic religion deeply, recognizes that they had a Mother once. They either miss Her, or they are terrified that She is coming back.

The denial of the Feminine has not exactly been consistent, even within Christianity. So the Gynarchist scholar of religion might take note, that if one wants to find the Divine Feminine, even within Christianity itself, She is there.

> *"God loves all of us," she says, "and She wants us to know that She has changed Her garment merely. She is beyond female and male. She is beyond human understanding. But She calls your attention to that which you have forgotten. Jews: look to Miriam, not Moses, for what you can learn from her. Muslims: look to Fatima, not Muhammad. Buddhists: remember Tara, the mother of liberation. Christians: pray to Mary for your salvation."*

— Naomi Alderman, *The Power*

Mary Magdalene

The apostles were privy to the fact that Mary Magdalene had been Jesus's favorite. In fact, while affirming her special status, some expressed their disdain.

From the Gospel of Philip:

> *"And the companion of the [saviour was] Mary Magdalene. [Christ] loved Mary more than [all] the disciples, [and used to] kiss her [often] on the [mouth]. The rest of the disciples [were offended by it and expressed disapproval]. They said to him, "Why do you love her more than all of us?" The Saviour answered and said to them, "Why do I not love you like her? When a blind man and one who sees are both together in darkness, they are no different from one another. When the light comes, then he who sees will see the light, and he who is blind will remain in darkness."*

Mary claimed that Jesus had given her secret teachings. The *Gospel of Mary Magdalene* was found in the *Berlin Gnostic Codex* discovered in the late 19th Century in upper Egypt. It was likely copied and bound between the fourth and fifth centuries CE. And it includes the teachings that Jesus shared with Mary.

There's an interesting passage in Chapter 9, which illustrates a bit of the misogyny Mary faced.

> *"4) He questioned them about the Savior: Did He really speak privately with a woman and not openly to us? Are we to turn about and all listen to her? Did He prefer her to us?*
>
> *5) Then Mary wept and said to Peter, My brother Peter, what do you think? Do you think that I have thought this up myself in my heart, or that I am lying about the Savior?*

6) Levi answered and said to Peter, Peter you have always been hot tempered.

7) Now I see you contending against the woman like the adversaries.

8) But if the Savior made her worthy, who are you indeed to reject her? Surely the Savior knows her very well.

9) That is why He loved her more than us. Rather let us be ashamed and put on the perfect Man, and separate as He commanded us and preach the gospel, not laying down any other rule or other law beyond what the Savior said."

Many of the apostles were not too fond of listening to women. Paul would also go on to say that women should be silent. In 1 Corinthians 14:

"the women should keep silent in the churches. For they are not permitted to speak, but should be in submission, as the Law also says.

And if they desire to learn anything, let them ask their own husbands at home; for it is improper for a woman to speak in church."

One can admire the character of Mary for bearing the burden of being the savior's confidant and a keeper of mysteries, amongst a band of men who resented her and thought women to be of lesser importance. Her gender is likely why her gospel was excluded from the canonical Bibles we read today.

But beyond the existence of such an important female figure who had direct access to the savior, there were other early Christians who revered a Mother figure over the old testament god.

The Gnostics

> "During the first three centuries of Christianity, there was no central authority until after the conversion of Roman emperor Constantine the Great in 312 CE. Christian communities taught many different views. In the 2nd century CE, some groups, now collectively referred to as Gnostic Christians, claimed to have access to 'secret knowledge' about the nature of the universe, the nature of Christ, and what his appearance on earth meant to believers. In the middle of the 2nd century CE, a group of Christian leaders retroactively referred to as the Church Fathers (Justin Martyr, Irenaeus, Tertullian, and others) wrote volumes against these Gnostic Christians." (Denova)

It's worth noting that the concepts of orthodoxy and heresy were invented just for them. They called the Old Testament god the "demiurge," and they saw him as a kind of bastard child of the divine being Sophia (which also means wisdom). In their version of things, this demiurge did create the earth, but it wasn't a very good place. Sophia had to lend her divine spark in order for humans to be created. We all have her spark within us, but we've forgotten. To many of these early Christians, the god of Abraham had a single mom, and he was trouble - he was not only evil but Satan himself. And, of course, he didn't want humans to know about Her or their own divine spark as they would be harder to control.

The Demiurge - the God of the Old Testament according to Gnostics

Christ, the logos, arrived to remind humans of who and what they are and to get them in touch with their divinity. He wanted to save us, to help us escape this worldly prison through gnosis or knowledge. And so he was persecuted. Some Gnostics think of Christ as an avatar or manifestation of Sophia, and there are still churches today devoted to Her. According to Gnostics, Her origin seems to be in a larger deity or presence which holds the powerful potential of all life but is passive and uninvolved, reflecting the Shiva/Shakti paradigm.

But the Church really didn't like this story. Constantine I ordered the Gnostic texts to be destroyed, but some were copied and hidden. Some were saved and buried at Nag Hammadi, which are now referred to as the Nag Hammadi Library. Gnostics went underground and resurfaced again about a thousand years later, and their teachings were part of the reason for the Inquisition. A group of Gnostic Christians called Cathars were burned at the stake in a mass genocide.

A Gynarchist who may want to hold onto their Christian heritage may take an interest in Gnosticism and find out what Jesus was really trying to accomplish in saving humankind. They may find the Divine Feminine in Sophia and the apostle Mary Magdalene.

What about the Virgin Mary?

Another aspect of the Divine Feminine, of course, is Mary, the Mother of Christ. In fact, in some places, where Catholicism reigns, the Mother seems to be venerated even more than the Son. There are entire churches devoted to Her. The cult of the Virgin Mary has many adherents.

> *"Mary embodied many of the ideals of courtly love, intro-*
> *duced at the time of the Cult of Chivalry and practiced*

during the Medieval period. She was pure, free of sin, and the perfect mother. Imagery began to appear, statues were placed in churches, showing the Virgin with her child, countless roadside shrines where people could stop and pray, tokens and amulets with her image upon them to ward off all manner of illnesses and disease. Women prayed to her to help them conceive or watch over their children. Crusaders returned with Mary relics and carried images and symbols of the Virgin upon their banners, this then spilled over onto the field of jousting tournaments."
(HLB)

Collyridianism was an early Christian movement of women in Arabia that viewed Mary as a Goddess equated with Isis. It is common in cases where Christianity was forcefully adopted on top of existing indigenous religions, that the people give their previous gods the names of saints and continue to go right on worshiping them. You can see this clearly in the Afro-Caribbean religions commonly called Voodoo and Santeria. It's a covert way for cultures to maintain their devotions and traditions without facing religious persecution. In a similar fashion, though Jesus was born in the Spring, Christians celebrate his birth near the Winter solstice when indigenous religions celebrated the birth of the sun. Easter, celebrating the resurrection, falls near the Spring Equinox - a time of rebirth across most of human cultures. It seems our ancient nature-based rituals persist no matter what the religion.

The Druids

I often wonder why those with European heritage forsake the perfectly wonderful traditions of their ancient ancestors to cling to the Middle Eastern mythology and religion of Christianity. But, of course, the most likely answer lies in the Romans, and Christianity's mission to conquer the world. And it often has done so by force, through crusades and colonization. This is the unfortunate fate of a defeated people. Our native cultures are too often destroyed or driven into hiding.

There are some who have bravely carried on their traditions in secret or revived them after a long period of stasis.

> The Druids were suppressed in Gaul by the Romans under Tiberius (reigned 14–37 CE) and probably in Britain a little later. In Ireland they lost their priestly functions after the coming of Christianity and survived as poets, historians, and judges (filid, senchaidi, and brithemain). Many scholars believe that the Hindu Brahman in the East and the Celtic Druid in the West were lateral survivals of an ancient Indo-European priesthood. (Bauer)

Druids were responsible for organizing worship and sacrifices, divination, and judicial procedure in Gallic, British, and Irish societies. Their texts were committed to memory and passed down in oral tradition, even though they were thought to be a literate group. We do know that they believed in reincarnation, with the human soul being indestructible, entering the body of a new infant after the death of their old body. Many Druids were women, and there was no power imbalance between them and their male counterparts.

Anu or Danu (a contraction of Dia Anu) is the oldest of the Celtic Gods and is thought of as the Mother God, giving birth to all the others. She has possible parallels with the Welsh Dôn in the medieval tales of the *Mabinogion*, whom most modern scholars consider to be a mythological Mother Goddess. A tribe of supernatural beings called the Tuatha Dé Danann or "folk of Danu" dwell in the otherworld and interact with the human world. There are Celtic shamanic-like practices that involve humans journeying to the otherworld as well. These could be related to non-ordinary states of consciousness as described in the Psychology chapter.

Neo-Druid revivalism became popular in the 18th and 19th centuries. In 2010 Druidry became an officially recognized religion in the U.K. As the neo-Druid religion is focused on humans' intimate relationship with nature, the Gynarchist could very easily feel at home in this tradition.

Hinduism

While the history of Judeo-Christian expansion was happening, people on the Indian continent were holding onto rich and varied regional religions, which, with the arrival of the British, were all lumped into the catch-all term Hinduism. Hindu became synonymous with "from India." The umbrella religion of India is more accurately referred to as Sanātana Dharma (the eternal way or eternal law). And the many sects of Buddhism branched off from this. The Divine Feminine never left India, making it the culture with the longest-lasting continuous worship of Goddesses (aka, Devi) on earth. Every village in India, in fact, has its own resident Goddess.

It is for this reason that the central religious beliefs and practices of Gynarchy take on Sanskrit names like Devi, Bhakti, Nandi, Dasa, and Seva, to honor this unbroken tradition (see "a note on the appropriation of language" in the section on the Devi Doctrine). Having had time to evolve naturally without interruption, Indian belief systems are some of the most sophisticated systems of thought in human history. They have inspired great physicists like Bohr, Schrödinger, Oppenheimer, and Heisenberg to take on fresh perspectives regarding the workings of the universe.

The Indian philosophy of most interest to the Gynarchist is Trika, or Kashmir Shaivism. It is a non-dualist belief system, meaning that Devi is not one half of a whole, but She is the unpaired Creatrix of all things, who emerged from the unmanifest absolute silent state of Siva. She is one and the same, just in an active state. All things are in fact Devi Herself, as she creates endless new aspects of Herself in order to understand Herself fully. In reality, there is nothing but Devi. We are made by Devi, and we are Her. This is the conception of divinity most analogous to the core spiritual teachings of Gynarchy. Abhinavagupta was known as the tradition's most important thinker, and the Tantraloka is his most important work. Tantra means the weave, composition, or continuity (of the universe), and loka is to shine a light.

Another Hindu-turned-Buddhist concept is that of the Living Goddess. In India, it has never been unusual for a realized woman to set up a temple for Herself and act as either

Guru, Saint, or Goddess, providing counsel and blessings, and offering Darshan (beholding the deity) to the people around her. Contemporary Indian spiritual leader Sadhguru talks of his grandmother, who did so in her 60s, and continued to take on that role until she died at age 113.

There are many Female saints and gurus, from Amma, the hugging saint, to Mother Meera, an Avatar of Devi.

> *"The Divine Mother has always been worshiped as the sustaining soul force of the universe. Although some of the faces she wears are well-known - Kali, The Virgin Mary, Isis, for example - some of Her embodied forms have chosen to work quietly in the world. In turbulent times such as these, several incarnations of the Divine Mother move among us, each with Her particular task of healing or protection, or transformation."* Mother Meera, March 2001

In Nepal, the Kumari are living embodiments of the Goddess Telaju. They are young girls who spend a portion of their lives before puberty receiving puja - ritual offering and devotion in Temples in and around the Kathmandu Valley. At puberty, when they are done, they return to their lives as regular women and new Kumari are found to take their place. They are consecrated human beings taking on the role of deity to connect with devotees.

Along the same lines, the concept of the Dakini has evolved in Buddhism. All women can be seen as some kind of Dakini manifestation. The Dakini embodies both humanity and deity in human form. A Dakini is fierce, playful, nurturing, wrathful, and peaceful. She is the flow of energy the yogic practitioner must work with to evolve, and She changes her qualities depending on the situation and the need of the moment. The Dakini guards the secrets of spiritual practice and reveals them when the practitioner is ready. They were at one time considered demonic, as fierce-looking female embodiments of enlightened energy and wisdom.

In Indian religion, all forms and manifestations of Devi are considered Mulaprakriti; Literally, the root or origin of nature; primary cause or originant; original root of which matter or all apparent forms are evolved. They are not created; they are creation itself.

Taoism

As we move further East, we find still other unique belief systems. Taoism refers to Chinese philosophy, or a set of religions that emphasize harmony with the Tao, or "the Way," which is the source of all things and the underlying principle of all that exists. It was typically passed on from master to disciple, and its roots can be traced back to prehistoric China.

Much like Siva, The Tao is indescribable and transcends analysis and definition. It can only be witnessed via the results of its presence in the rhythmic processes and patterns in nature. One knows one is aligned with the Tao when there is "action without action" - a kind of effortlessness called wu wei.

Qi is the vital energy or "breath" of life, and, somewhat like Shakti, it is the material force of the universe. Death is the dispersal of Qi. Through Qi cultivation, one can improve health, live a long life, and even obtain magical powers and immortality. You may have noted the description of the White Tigress in our roles within Gynarchy. A White Tigress is a female Daoist Master who collects Qi from men through sex. This helps her to promote social harmony and extend her lifespan, possibly indefinitely. Immortals called Xians are able to come and go from the mortal realm at will and can teach others how to become immortal.

Livia Kohn explains the basic Daoist cosmological theory as follows:

> "The root of creation Dao rested in deep chaos (ch. 42). Next, it evolved into the One, a concentrated state of cosmic unity that is full of creative potential and often described in Yijing terms as the Great Ultimate (Taiji). The One then brought forth "the Two," the two energies yin and yang, which in turn merged in harmony to create the next level of existence, "the Three" (yin-yang combined), from which the myriad beings came forth. From original oneness, the world thus continued to move into ever greater states of distinction and differentiation."

This may bring to mind the oldest creation myth, where the Goddess of all emerges from chaos, creates duality, and procreates with the serpent (representing knowledge of herself) in order to create the egg of the universe from which everything is hatched. Here we begin to understand some worldwide themes which can help us begin to piece together a common human religion.

The Akan

The Akan people are a large meta-ethnic group in Africa who trace their lineage back to the original woman, their collective grandmother, Onyame. They call this matrilineal organization Ebusua. The Akan evoke spirits, and divinities called abosom and can become possessed by them. They dance and sing songs to remind people of much-needed lessons. Some are ancient and eternal. Some are ancestors.

In Akan philosophy, there is an infinite, indescribable source called Nyankopon. It has no attributes, and they do not pray to it, but it is present in every living thing. This is very similar to the concept of Siva in Trika. The gods, divinities, and humans emerged from Nyankopon. Asase Ya is a possible parallel to Devi, the Feminine creative energy. She is the great female spirit of the earth, governing the fertility of land and animals and creativity.

When the Akan die, they believe people of good moral character enter the abode of the ancestors called Asamando. Those who do not lead a life of merit have to return, being reincarnated in order to try again. A person of bad moral character is termed "not a person." To be a "real person," you have to live ethically. Social status and wealth have no bearing on this personhood. Only actions and character. Prayers can be made to the ancestors for assistance. Liberation happens when the ancestors return to the infinite source Nyonkopon and become free of differences.

The complexity and richness of the religions of Africa make them a fascinating topic of study for the Gynarchist scholar, as it may give us insight into what we might call the original religion. Human life began in Africa, as did ideas about our origins, and the blueprint of our existence.

The Atheist and the Jew

In my lifelong theological studies, I discovered an interesting correlation between atheism and the earliest iterations of Judaism. At the religion's inception, Jewish philosophy conveyed the idea that god created the Earth according to a set of rules, and he put humans on "the Good Earth" to be a kind of conscious witness to creation (because what's the point of creating something cool if there's no one there to see it?). Earth was a place of awe and marvels, and we were just lucky to be here at all. The idea was that, when humans died, our bodies were put in the ground and that our consciousness or soul - the thing that makes us animate and aware - went into a deep and unending sleep where we don't think, feel, or experience anything at all until the end of time. Death is the end, and after that, there's nothing. Final rest. The best thing is to stay alive as long as possible on Earth because this is it. You get one life to live in the best way you can. The idea of life after death was Greek to the early Jew (quite literally, as the idea came from the Greeks, not the Torah).

This sense of finding wonder in our very existence, in the mundane yet miraculous fact that we are here at all, is shared between atheism and the early Abrahamic religion. And perhaps, even if we wake up and dream that there must be much more to the story than that, we should carry that sense of wonder with us. Because this place called Earth is quite a spectacle to behold.

...

It would be impossible to cover all of the world's religions in one chapter, so I tried to concentrate on the oldest and most prominent and provide an overview of their cosmology and common themes. There have been many new religions and spiritual practices which have gained traction, like Baha'i, Kabbalah, Rosicrucians, Sikhism, Wicca, and the like, but most are just remixes or revivals of older ideas.

What becomes clear when studying world religions is that there are some threads that are carried throughout human spiritual philosophy and practices. There are many names and configurations for similar ideas. Following those threads can help us have a perspective on the nature of the universe.

And though many of the Abrahamics have made, and still make, a concerted effort to squash the Feminine, like grass growing through cracks in the sidewalk, She inevitably works Her way back to the surface, even within their own system of beliefs. The Gynarchist always looks for points of connection through which to build alliances. Remember that it is quite normal for differing ideologies to coexist, as variety feeds wisdom. We can never expect or insist that everyone sees things as we do. Imagine how boring that would be. But when we stop viewing everything through the lens of competition, difference need never mean conflict.

| 3-6 |

SOCIOLOGY

As we form our Hives, it's helpful to look at how groups organize themselves. What are different kinds of relationships which may exist within Gynarchy? What do family and community structures look like? And how do we apply the Pillars of Gynarchy to the shape of our world?

> *"So pickled is the male creation with the vinegar of Authoritarianism, that even those who have gone further and repudiated the State still cling to the god, Society as it is, still hug the old theological idea that they are to be 'heads of the family.'"* Voltairine DeCleyre

Family

The nuclear family, mom and dad, and a few kids, once the ideal of the mid-20th century, presents a lot of problems.

The isolation it engenders keeps us dependent on a partner or parent for most of our practical and emotional needs. This often leads to periods of emotional neglect. As adults, if we attach our sense of security to our sexual partner, this creates sexual dysfunction as it can generate a feeling of obligation to engage in sex in order to maintain safety and emotional support. Worse yet, some partners will actively withhold or withdraw affection if their sexual needs are not served.

It's uncommon to be able to afford the cost of living on one income as it was in the past. With two exhausted parents, the division of labor gets tricky and is a source of tension. Even when single-income families were the norm, the job of the mother was a 24/7 365 arrangement, often leading to burnout and the use of alcohol and medications ("Mother's Little Helpers") to be able to tolerate the strain. Physical and sexual abuse by parents or siblings is also more likely to go unnoticed or unreported when it happens inside nuclear families.

Though referred to as "traditional," this nuclear setup is far from the common family structure of our ancestors. It's quite unusual, in fact. It came about after the Second World War, deliberately promoted by some governments to get women out of the labor force and ensure jobs for returning service-men. Television, magazines, and advertisements reinforced the image, stamping it on our consciousness as "normal." The only groups who do reasonably well in nuclear families are very high-income families who outsource domestic labor and childcare to paid help. And even so, both the adults and children in the family need an active and intimate social network in order to get their needs met.

Pair bonding is natural in humans who create a child together, but that pair bond has not always been permanent, and it hasn't even always meant cohabitation of the two parents (in some matriarchies, the woman stays with her close female relatives and the father of her child lives elsewhere). Research shows that more cooperative models of raising children has historically had the most advantages, both in terms of shared labor and the development of cognitive ability in our offspring. This means a household with extended family members to share the domestic, childcare, and financial responsibilities, as well as friends and family outside the home who take a regular interest in the children and have close bonds with the adults.

The more interactions a child has with a number of loving and invested caregivers of varying ages and personalities, the better the child's brain develops and the more prosocial behaviors and less anxiety they exhibit into adulthood. They also have greater support and people to turn to when they are struggling, and there are fewer instances of neglect. In early childhood, before age five, a close bond with the mother is, of course, essential. But it doesn't need to be exclusive, and as the child grows, they benefit more from a network of care. It gives them a sense of belonging and identity. Ever hear the saying, "It takes a village?" In the case of Gynarchy, it takes a Hive. Children are happier when brought up by a number of responsible and engaged adults, and Women are always much happier and less stressed when they are not the only ones looking after their children.

Relationships

It should be pretty obvious that Female Led Relationships, or FLRs, are the norm within a Gynarchy. This means the woman selects her partner or partners, sets the rules and expectations of the relationship, and she has the final say in all important matters. In Gynarchy, women have the authority.

But the shape of these relationships can vary widely, from monogamous pairs to whole harems of men serving one woman. And not even men are expected to be bonded to one woman alone in all cases. Letting go of the idea that all intimate relationships need to be monogamous brings a sense of relief to some. Knowing what relationship style you feel most comfortable and fulfilled in helps you pick the right partner or partners. Some potential relationship orientations include:

The Monogamous Couple: Two people who are happiest concentrating on one another to the exclusion of all other potential romantic or sexual partners.

The Cuckoldress: A woman who is free to have sexual and possibly romantic relations with whomever she pleases but also has a singularly devoted male who serves and engages with her exclusively.

The Unattached Woman: A woman who may accept the services of all kinds from the men in the Hive but doesn't wish to solidify a serious romantic or sexual attachment with anyone.

The Unattached Man: A man devoted to serving any and all women of his Hive in a variety of ways, without belonging to any one Woman.

The Shared Man: A man who is shared as a personal servant, devotee, and/or partner in a completely open and friendly agreement between two or more Women. They may each have a uniquely different relationship with him.

The Lesbian Triad: Two female romantic partners who have adopted a male servant as exclusively their own.

The Harem: A woman with multiple male partners and/or servants, who are bonded to her exclusively and belong to her alone, usually without romantic or sexual attachments to each other or outside the harem.

The Polycule: A small group of any gender combination who are committed to only having sexual and romantic encounters and attachments within their chosen group.

The Queen's Court: When all of a Hive's members develop a romantic and/or sexual commitment to the Queen exclusively, though dalliances among the members of the court may be pre-approved or arranged by the Queen Herself or organized as parties and orgies.

Marriage

Some will have a sentimental attachment to the idea of

marriage. It's programmed into our brains from an early age that marriage is the romantic ideal and the outward signal of success for a happy relationship. Meanwhile, at least half of all marriages end in divorce.

In Gynarchy, it is seen as beneficial to take any relationship contract in stages.

1. *A three-month trial* - use this time to get to know each other without getting serious or exclusive in any way. I recommend avoiding any and all sexual activity during this period as it interferes with one's judgment (I will explain more about the seven-year sexual link in a later chapter but suffice it to say you may want to avoid it at this early stage). You should not underestimate the pleasure of longing. This is the stage where you begin to negotiate what your ideal relationship might look like.

2. *A one-year contract* - usually with expectations outlined in writing. After one year, the partners assess if they want to continue on.

3. *A three or five-year contract* - Similar to the one-year contract but using the experiences of the first contract to iron out the details of any rules, protocols, and expectations, and make a longer commitment to one another.

4. *An indefinite contract* - This contract can still be broken if things go wrong. But it's an indication to both

partners that the intent is to commit to staying together for the long term unless and until one or both have the strong desire to end the contract. A man may be permanently marked with a tattoo or the like to show his commitment to the contract.

There can be, if the partners wish it, ceremonies in front of the whole Hive or among friends and family for each of these stages in order to publicly celebrate their relationship. But notice I didn't mention marriage. A Woman is certainly free to marry whomever she wants if that is Her desire. But, first, there are some things to consider about the institution of marriage itself.

My namesake Voltairine DeCleyre was a freethinker opposed to marriage back in 1907. First, she saw it as an unwarranted interjection of church or state, or both, into the private lives of two people. Secondly, she saw it as a killer of love.

> *"Nowadays I would say that I prefer to see a marriage based purely on business considerations, than a marriage based on love. That is not because I am in the least concerned with the success of the marriage, but because I am concerned with the success of love. And I believe that the easiest, surest and most applicable method of killing love is marriage."* Voltairine DeCleyre

She thought marriage also tended to inhibit the full realization of the individual as an autonomous being, and that the world would be better off with more unmarried people, free from convention and also free from raising children. On the first count, at least, I do know those who have lost their sense of self within marriage, myself among them. Finding yourself bending your psyche in unnatural directions just to make a relationship last is not good for anyone. I rediscovered my authentic desires and motivations upon divorce.

DeCleyre's arguments have merit, but other objections may go back to the history of marriage. Once upon a time, women were treated as chattel, and all marriages were arranged marriages. The tradition of the father walking the bride to the altar was all about handing off property from one man to another. Dowry was thrown in to sweeten the deal.

Also, the whole garter ritual was about making sure the couple consummated the marriage in order to start making heirs so that family lines would continue unbroken. Children were an asset because they provided free labor when they got old enough to work on the farm or family business. At one time, family members would watch the couple get it on and then bring out an article of the bride's undergarments to prove their union to the waiting crowd. The symbolic garter removal by the groom came to replace this tradition.

In parts of the world, like Kyrgyzstan, the tradition of bride kidnapping is still popular, and two-thirds of those are non-consensual. This practice has existed since the founding of Rome, and English brides could be victims of it until it was outlawed in England in 1753. The original role of the "Best Man" was to assist in the abduction and make sure the bride did not escape.

Today, one can find videos of women protesting as they

are abused and coerced by the man's family into accepting their kidnapper's marriage proposal. They may already have boyfriends and are still forced into situations where they become sex slaves and provide offspring and domestic labor for the man. Mock kidnappings celebrating this tradition are still a part of wedding ceremonies in some parts of Eastern Europe.

It's this sort of ritualized use of women as tradable objects, slaves, and baby factories that might give marriage the stink of patriarchy that won't wash off and could put the Gynarchist off from engaging in the tradition. Of course, if the groom is amenable, a woman might want to pull a full reversal and enact mock revenge on behalf of her ancestors and all women who had to endure such humiliation. Whatever the case, we should go into any such ritual or ceremony with the full knowledge of its implications. Marriage does not have to be the sole symbol of a successful committed relationship.

Naming Conventions

In patriarchal culture, a woman is given her father's surname at birth to mark her as his child, and then she changes that upon marriage to indicate that she belongs to her husband. In Gynarchy, it is a natural rite of passage for a woman to choose her own name, and legally change it upon entering a Hive or reaching adulthood.

Name affirmation ceremonies are held to celebrate coming into one's own. And if a woman particularly loves the name her parents gave her, she may simply reaffirm it as her chosen name. But if she wishes to break the patrilineal line of ownership, she is encouraged to choose a surname of a more feminine origin. Usually, it will be the *first* name of a female relative, a woman she admires, or a significant woman in history. If not a family name, it is a sign of spiritual lineage. It will *not* be that woman's last name (at least not for a generation or two), as that is still a patrilineal name.

Sarah Smith may become Sarah Victoria or Sarah Fatima. And beyond that, she is encouraged to change her first, middle, and last names entirely if she is not fond of them, and she should never be afraid to choose names from nature or unusual and original names. Creativity is a trait to be admired. I changed my entire name and took the surname Voltairine in honor of anarchist feminist Voltairine DeCleyre.

A man may keep his given name or choose to petition his Queen or a Female partner to rename him to Her liking. She may give him either Her chosen last name or Her first name as his surname or choose to give him no surname at all. Though it is considered an *immense* honor to be renamed by a woman, and a point of real pride to carry the name she has given, he is also permitted to choose his own name if he prefers.

Living Arrangements

It is important that every member of the Hive have a private living space of their own of some kind, even if they spend most of their time with a partner. This can be a private bedroom in a large house, hotel, or inn. It can be separate apartments, or even separate houses in a village, or cabins on the same estate or compound. It might be that a fledgling Hive starts out living separately within the same city with common meeting spaces, and then pools their resources to acquire their collective home.

The ability to spend time alone, away from everyone, helps to make communal living go much more smoothly. It's hard to know oneself if one cannot spend time alone with oneself. And even when people pair up, they may need time independent from one another, or they may separate at some point and won't want to be stuck sleeping in the same bed. Not to mention there may be issues like snoring, differing schedules, or preferring to have the covers all to yourself, which may make even closely bonded partners prefer their own sleeping quarters. The right to privacy goes hand in hand with the right to autonomy.

Living in close proximity, either through co-housing or creating a village or town, makes the division of labor and resources much easier and is a financial benefit to all. Having ample accommodations for everyone, including plenty of storage space in the kitchen, enough washers and dryers for all members to access when needed, and plenty of bathroom facilities reduces tension within the group.

There should be rituals in place to acclimate each new member to the community, as outlined in a future chapter. And the assignment of tasks should be centralized, public, and utilize each member's strengths. Unpleasant jobs should be shared and scheduled so as not to become the burden of one person alone. We should take advice from other success-ful intentional communities to avoid common pitfalls.

Some examples of well-established communities to learn from:

> **Damanhur** - *The central part of Damanhur is located between Turin and Aosta, in an uncontaminated valley at the foot of the Piedmont Alps in Italy. The six-hundred citizens who live there have created a multilingual society, open to exchanges with the world and the different cultures of peoples. Many other Damanhurians live in other parts of Italy and all over the world and support the Federation's ideals and projects.*
>
> *In 1975, together with a group of fellow researchers, Falco Tarassaco started the social and spiritual experiment of Damanhur. The Federation now has its own Constitution, a complementary currency system called "Credito," schools for children, art studios, a publishing house, an organic farm and a renowned medical center for holistic therapies.*
>
> *Most impressive are their underground Temples of Humankind, magnificent works of art dug into the mountain by hand by the first citizens of Damanhur. They proceeded without permits, and, when the police raided, they saw the awesome beauty of the place and it was decided that the Temples were too magnificent to be shut down. They contain the history of the spiritual life of the planet.*

The Bruderhof - *There are more than 20 Bruderhof locations around the world, which include large villages, apartment complexes in cities, and single shared homes. They are a Christian group who try to live as early Christians did in communal settings with no one member owning property or possessions, and everyone's work being valued equally.*

"Founded in 1920, our community was one of many that sprang up in Germany after World War I among young people disillusioned with a society based on competition and greed and a church that had blessed the war. Eberhard Arnold, his wife Emmy, and a circle of fellow seekers left middle-class Berlin to start a rural settlement in the spirit of early Christianity and the Radical Reformation of the early 1500s, when thousands of Anabaptists left the institutional churches to live a life of sharing and service in Christian communities."

"Membership requires a voluntary lifetime commitment, so it is a choice that can only be made as an adult. Those who grow up in the community are encouraged to spend time elsewhere so they can make a mature, independent choice. Work is love made visible. From washing clothes in the communal laundry or teaching in the school, to weighing a baby in the community clinic or fixing a water main, our communal work is a practical expression of our love

for one another. No one receives a wage or salary. We earn our living by manufacturing and selling Community Playthings (classroom furniture and play equipment)."

Findhorn - *Findhorn Ecovillage was founded in 1985 in Scotland from a simple caravan park started in the 1960s. They have a number of businesses, shops, and non-profits with over 400 residents, and more than 3000 people from around the world taking part in the residential programs each year.*

"The Findhorn Ecovillage is a tangible demonstration of the links between the spiritual, social, ecological, and economic aspects of life and is a synthesis of some of the very best of current thinking on human habitats. It is a constantly evolving model used as a teaching resource by a number of university and school groups as well as by professional organisations and municipalities worldwide."

Those are just a few from a long list of examples of communities that have thrived over the past century by intentionally coming together around shared values and a shared vision. It shows what is possible when people feel strongly about creating a world in which they are happy to live.

Of course, it is idealistic to think that that's all it takes. Hives should learn from failed communities of the past, as well as those who succeed. We have enough examples behind us to discover common issues and themes that each Hive should keep in mind.

Co-housing groups of more than 24 people make it difficult to maintain intimacy. Groups less than 12 do not have enough shared resources and labor to add ease to each other's lives. So co-housing situations should be kept to 12-24 individuals under the same roof. If a Hive grows to over 108 people, there should definitely be more than one Queen.

We should also be mindful of the so-called "Dunbar number." In a 1993 paper, Robin Dunbar estimated, based on primate behavior and the size of the human brain, that functional human social groups max out at around 150 members. These are the number of people we can know well enough to recognize, know their personality and know how they are related to other members of the group. And when he looked at every group from Neolithic villages, tribes, communes, and army units, they all maxed out around the same number. When our numbers increase beyond this, one Hive needs to split off into multiple related Hives. Governments fail because they become too large to manage the interests of all their citizens. We are not interested in building large bureaucracy-filled governments.

In the past, there have also been cases where a new community attracts 500 members all at once, but only 150 have any usable skills, and 50 have the emotional capacity to be empathetic and supportive of their fellow members. It would be a mistake to accept everyone who expresses an interest. It should be stressed that Hives do not want freeloading dreamers or those who do not play well with others. This is why the roles are outlined as they are. Each member needs to bring something of practical use to the Hive, be it skills, knowledge, labor or money.

Any new residents of the Hive need to undergo a trial period, just as partners do in intimate relationships. This can be a few weeks or a few months, but until they have found their functional place in the community, they should be considered temporary residents. And when they finally officially become a member of the Hive, there should be a celebration.

Likewise, remembering the Pillar of Consent, children must affirm their intent to stay within our Hives, or within the broader network of Gynarchy, when they become adults. They are encouraged to experience other ways of living until they decide if Gynarchy is a way of life they authentically embrace. One of the biggest failings of communities in the past has been isolationism. The most successful and long-lasting Hives will have active involvement outside their bubble, participating in the broader social and economic system around them.

Judiciary Methods

Every Hive should have its own official constitution wherein the expectations and rights of its members are clearly stated. This can be periodically reviewed and amended and should be clear and simple enough that there are no misunderstandings. Those who repeatedly violate the Hive's constitution should be ousted. Think of it as weeding the garden.

All conflict may be resolved by the Queen or Oracles, or, in more democratic Hives, a Congress of the Women. Using the Pillar of Conflict Resolution, Women will become especially practiced at the skills of locating, approving, and influencing, as well as uncovering the underlying needs of all parties involved. A formal system of complaint and resolution should be put into place.

But sometimes, there are shadows afoot and undiscovered and unspoken drama within people that needs to be excavated. In such cases, arguments and disagreements can also be dealt with through play. Bullying is not tolerated, but imagine conflicts being addressed through Queen-sanctioned mock battles between groups, or duels with paint guns. In untenable situations where it can't be decided who is right or wrong, invent games where the winner of the game gets a judgment in their favor. Satisfy the masculine inclination for competition through good-natured sport. In kinky Hives, if someone has repeatedly broken the rules or protocols, perhaps a public flogging would be in order.

If you've ever had the opportunity to work with autistic children, you know that they can be prone to meltdowns when their emotions become dysregulated. They may cry, hit themselves, rage, and become quite violent. Aside from giving them space and taking attention away from the behavior, one of the most effective ways to help them interrupt the cycling chaos and regulate those overwhelming feelings is to put on silly voices and become different characters - to play! Neurotypical adults are embarrassed to admit that this is just a more exaggerated version of what happens inside all our heads when things are not going our way.

One resource to look to for the validity of exercising the demons of conflict is Alejandro Jodorowsky and his book *Psychomagic.* He speaks of creating cracks in the expected and ordinary in order to let out the stuff that is trapped within and pressurized. So much can be shaken up and revealed in theatrical-style improvisation. When there is human drama in social situations, sometimes it just needs to be given an outlet to play out as just that - drama. It needs a stage, an audience, and a beginning, middle, and end. And when we are unable to work logically, we must immerse ourselves in metaphor, stories, and poetry in order to resolve issues. It's a skill innate to all humans as small children, but we too often lose as we grow into adults.

Never ever forget that the Feminine is playful! The more absurd and memorable the event, the greater our bonds and the higher our spirits. We need never invalidate the needs and desires of our community members, but if we take ourselves too seriously, we can spiral into adversarial relationships and misery. Sometimes we will need to be reminded of just that.

| 3-7 |

SEX EDUCATION

Basics

It is a sad fact that some boys go around thinking that women pee from their vaginas. First and foremost, a basic understanding of the sexual anatomy of all humans should be taught from an early age. There should be no shame in knowing the parts of the body and their functions. We should leave no one guessing in this regard. Adults who missed these lessons need to be brought up to speed.

Everyone should know how fertility and the menstrual cycle work and all the options for girls and women for handling their periods, from pads to cups to period panties, and all the ways in which she might relax and manage any discomfort. Menstrual products should be free and available in every restroom, and designated bathhouses for free bleeding should be readily available for use. Women should be able to take time off from their usual day-to-day responsibilities during their periods, just as our ancestors did.

The pros and cons of every type of birth control should be discussed at length, including the potential health problems brought on by the use of hormonal birth control. Abortion should be presented as a last resort option, along with ways to transform the process into a holy sacrament if a woman is ever in the unfortunate position of making such a choice. From the onset of sexual activity, methods of contraception should be freely available, and instructions on their use should be clear. Unwanted pregnancy is to be actively avoided.

Everyone should know about the mechanism of erections and know that sometimes boys and men become erect in a random fashion. An erection does not count as consent. They should know the delicate nature of the testicles and the protective function of the foreskin. In Gynarchy, any modifications of the sexual organs, from circumcision to vasectomies to castration, are to be done by a professional on consenting adults only. No man will be forced to be modified, nor will he be shamed if he elects to modify his body by choice. Children are not to be circumcised as they cannot consent, and the procedure comes with more potential risks and downsides than benefits. And adult males may choose to be sterilized or to become eunuchs if they so desire.

Energetics

Beyond the important basics that some of us were taught in school, about various STDs and pregnancy, anyone who's undergone puberty needs a basic grounding in human sexual relationships. This, of course, will mean a heavy emphasis on our pillars of Consent and Bodily Autonomy. Coercion is never tolerated. Everyone should clearly understand that an unconscious person cannot consent to sex, and that consent may be withdrawn at any point during a sexual encounter. Tips on creating safety and trust, reducing shame, and exploring one another's desires are also important. A sense of playfulness should replace any sense of shame around discussing desires and turn-ons.

Concepts of sexual, energetic cords should also be discussed. Depending upon the spiritual teacher, it is said that penetrative sex creates an energetic link between a man and woman which can last a year, or, some Buddhists say, up to seven years. Any and all alternatives to penetrative sex should be taught as immensely pleasurable options that help avoid this entanglement if you do not intend it. In fact, oral sex on the woman, and the use of hands and toys is highly encouraged in Gynarchy. But we should also teach women how to perform what's referred to as "cord cutting" so that they may end the energetic connection for themselves and other women when they have mistakenly attached to someone.

Libido

Everyone in Gynarchy should be taught ways in which to deal with unmatched libidos. Males with higher libidos than their partners should be either put into chastity or instructed to engage in a healthy amount of masturbation (a healthy amount means the amount that takes care of the sense of urgency without becoming compulsive). In rare exceptions, men with high libidos who are also highly artful and skilled lovers may be able to take on the role of sexual servants.

Though keep in mind, that the sexual servant is not concerned with his own orgasms. To be clear, every Gynarchist should know that the myth of blue balls is a blatant lie. Though frustrating and occasionally uncomfortable, being denied sex is not dangerous, and men are not harmed by abstaining. So men who beg, neg, nag, pout, pressure, haggle, manipulate, or coerce in order to get sex should be cut off completely and do not belong in our communities at all.

Women with higher libidos than their partners should be encouraged to get their needs met outside of the relationship through sexual servants, casual lovers, or multiple partners if that fits their relationship orientation, or learn to please themselves endlessly with toys if they wish to remain monogamous.

The Gynarchist knows that with the myriad of highly developed sex toys, women don't need a penis or a man to get off. Technology provides us with so many more (and often much better) outlets for our sexual needs. Building tension and devotion in men is fantastic! We should strive to cut off easy access to our bodies. Reduce pregnancies and drive away fuckboys, while still feeling the full potency of our erotic and orgasmic power. Hold a man off for three to six months, and then maybe see if he's good at oral sex. Make men work for it. Our pleasure is never dependent on them. To even touch us in sexual ways should be considered a privilege.

In short, masturbation is celebrated! However, we also respect that there may be asexual members of our hives for whom it may hold no interest. On the flip side of the coin, slut shaming is never tolerated. Myths around value and body count have no place in Gynarchy. Although penetrative sex may create an energetic connection, it does nothing to lower the inherent value of either person as a partner. Also, I think most people already know that sex doesn't "stretch out" a vagina or make it "loose." Women can give birth to whole humans, and it snaps back to its former size. Even a very big dick isn't going to have an effect, any more than a man having lots of intercourse would squeeze his penis, thereby causing it to shrink. The very idea that the male sex organ could take value away from a woman only shows that male ego and self-importance override their intelligence. If your dick is that disgustingly contaminated, perhaps it should be removed to save future sex partners from being diminished by it.

Porn

In Gynarchy, we realize not all porn is bad. Mainstream porn can be horribly exploitative and create misleading expectations around sex. We avoid those materials. Conscious porn made by women can be enjoyable, as well as fantasies created as animation and art without real human performers. As long as no one is hurt and no consent is violated, even extreme fantasy depictions would not be banned from our households and communities. Conscious consumption is key. FemDom porn is often a gateway drug to Gynarchy but should only be used with the understanding that it too can skew sexual expectations, which must then be adjusted to reality. Porn addiction can be dealt with if it impairs a man's functioning or becomes annoying to his partner. Resensitizing programs which involve meditation, sublimation, and semen retention are alchemical sexual tools to keep in our tool belts.

Endless Variety

It should be clear that every variation of human sexuality is embraced in Gynarchy, including homosexual and lesbian sex, bi and pan-sexuality, demi-sexuality, and asexuality. In fact, it seems obvious that many people fall somewhere in the middle of the hetero-homo spectrum, rather than on either end as fully straight or fully gay. This is a natural part of human sexuality.

Male chastity and pegging should be considered items on a healthy sexual menu, with detailed instructions on how to do both in the safest and more pleasurable fashion. Tantra, orgasm denial, edging, and non-ejaculatory orgasms should be topics of common knowledge.

Regarding BDSM: Kink, fetishes, and sadomasochism are natural and normal extensions of human sexual behavior rather than perversions. We often don't have much control over what turns us on, and sometimes arousal can be found in interesting places. We understand due to the unequal power dynamics in Gynarchy, it may attract more than a few people who only have an interest in kinky sex to the exclusion of vanilla sex. There are also some asexual or "graysexual" folks for whom kink is their only eroticism, and bumping uglies has no appeal. Kink is creative and playful and is driven by those essential qualities of the Feminine that are eager to experience all the sensations and explore fantasies that may stray far away from the typical.

"BDSM is childhood joyous play with adult sexual privilege and cool toys." Midori

FemDom in particular, expresses the direction of power native to Gynarchy: the Woman on top, commanding what She wants. It was from within the world of BDSM that I emerged with a greater understanding of my power, as have many other women.

Kink also can be used to create non-ordinary states of consciousness such as sub-space and the Dominant flow state. Aspects of kink can be used in powerfully transformative rituals and therapeutic processes. I have used it to help others release painfully stuck emotions. There's a lot of room within Gynarchy to explore these aspects of our erotic lives without guilt or shame.

Romance

I end this chapter with some advice I would offer to all women about sex and relationships. Take it (or leave it) as wisdom from an older sister or auntie.

A woman who seeks a male lover should seek him only for a temporary phase, so long as he brings her pleasure. For a woman who seeks a male partner, she should be ready to move on when the partnership no longer fulfills her, or if it pulls her away from her own desires and goals too much.

For the Queen or Lady who seeks a male devotee, she should find one or more who (even through any ups and downs with male lovers or perhaps even the longer stints with other partners) will make her happiness his ultimate priority, through every phase and era of her existence. Through every whim and every expansion, he should grow with her and adjust to her. He should listen and support her. A devotee is the most romantic of all F/m love relationships because he is true to her around every turn, her champion and confidant. He is completely invested and never jealous, gathering joy from her joy and pleasure from her pleasure, and multiplying it. He's the prince of compersion. He is not a sad and trampled doormat, but the proud trellis to her flowering vine - the core sacred masculine archetype. He's the witness and the buttress to her ceaseless growth. And if she should cast him aside, both would lose one of the most valuable relationships of their lives.

There are men who are cut out for this role, and who long for it. The cynical will name them "simps." But it is the closest thing to being one - in unity - with a woman that any man can ever dream of. It is an exalted position. Truly, there is nothing more *romantic* than the relationship between a Lady and her devotee.

| 3-8 |

FEMDOM AS RELIGION

[The following is a transcript from a lecture written for DomCon NOLA 2022, with a few notes pertaining to Gynarchy added in for cohesion. It was intended for an audience of FemDoms and avid BDSM practitioners.]

I'd like to make you aware of a momentum I am noticing, partially as a backlash to fundamentalist Christianity's intrusion into the laws of the U.S., of embracing the Feminine Divine. And I want to give you some history and context. But more than that, I want to inspire every woman reading this to understand that she can be a religious leader. We can use the effortlessly attractive and sacred structures of religion to our political advantage. We have the same kind of collective power as Evangelicals in that sense, and perhaps, if well organized, even more. I want you to know that every woman is capable of, and in fact built to, embody a Goddess, and to, in fact, become a Living Goddess in no uncertain terms.

That may seem pretty extreme or sacrilegious to some. But the time has come for women to embrace their very real power without coyness or hesitation.

I've noted that some Professional Dommes offer Goddess worship as part of their menu of professional services, and some may use it as part of their personal play, so we are already on our way. Sometimes we only need to hear someone grant us permission to take things further, and I am here to grant it. Each one of us is allowed to build our own damned temple! And what's more, we can network all our temples into a web that embraces the whole planet. If we can outnumber all the patriarchal preachers and pastors, we don't even need to fight, we can simply rob the patriarchy of the oxygen it needs to preach.

There is a popular Indian guru known as Sadhguru, and he talks about women as living goddesses, but he talks even more about his great-grandmother. She lived to be 113 years old, and people called her a wicked woman, not because she harmed anyone, but because her laugh could rock the whole neighborhood! In her 60s, when her husband died, she built a temple. And she did not install the statue of a deity at the center of it, but instead, she installed herself! I am making the bold suggestion that all of us who can embody the Divine Feminine have a duty to the world to install ourselves in our own temples. There have been some before us who have been so bold. I want to provide you with some examples.

My goal is to take you along on my own journey of surveying a number of very interesting women and groups in FemDom history. I owe a debt of gratitude to my friends Sylvie and Vixx. Sylvie and Vixx have embarked on the huge project of archiving as much FemDom history as humanly possible, collecting books, magazines, and scouring long-forgotten websites in order to preserve our rather fascinating past as women in kink. They've contributed a lot of knowledge and provided lots of new leads to follow.

So let me begin by sharing with you the criteria I used to define *what* I would refer to as "FemDom as Religion."

1. It is FemDom centered. This includes aspects of kink and/or themes of female supremacy. In short, Women are worshiped. Women explicitly dominate men and/or other women.
2. It has themes of Goddess/Dea worship. In order for it to be considered a religion for the sake of my survey, it needed to have one or more deities involved, and those deities need to be Feminine.
3. Organized into some sort of real-life group. This could be organized around a single woman and/or a common ideology of worship of the Feminine. Either way, it has to exist in real life, with real people, not just as a fantasy or fiction.

When I talk about FemDom as Religion, I am not necessarily talking about Sacred Kink, as written about by Lee Harrington in the book of the same name. Although you will find some serious cross-over in some instances. In the book, Harrington lays out the eightfold paths of BDSM. These include things like the Paths of Ritual, The Ascetic's Path, and The Ordeal Path. And you'll find, ritual, devotion, sacrifice, and ordeal are not uncommon to the practices I am about to describe. As Harrington points out, the eightfold paths of sacred kink show up in some form in every major religion in the world.

And I am not just talking about Goddess religions in general. My focus today is specifically on *female domination* within the context of the sacred. Meaning there are elements common to FemDom, like the worship of women, as well as things like discipline, humiliation and ego annihilation for men, and sadomasochistic practices.

I will touch briefly on my own mentor, Cleo Dubois's practices with her late husband, Fakir Musafar, who brought hook suspension and ritual piercing to the U.S. and were important to the modern primitive movement of BDSM. I will also draw your attention briefly to the Living Goddess traditions of India and Nepal, which though not related to BDSM, illustrate an important theme that I'd like to highlight - women worshiped as literal goddesses.

Some of the intriguing visionaries I'll tell you about today, and FemDom religions I'll cover:

- The Babalon Working of Marjorie Cameron in the 1940s-50s and how that has extended into contemporary times with the Red Goddess and Peter Grey's "becoming no man" rituals.
- The Service of Mankind Church started in 1979 to present.

- Aristasia from the 1980s, and the related temple of the Mother God.
- Guru Rasa, often seen stirring up trouble on daytime TV talk shows in the 1980s.
- The Cybelians, which began in 2004.
- The Universal Gynecocratic Republic, and their religion of Venus, active today.

Some of these unique thinkers may seem to you like crazed children playing out elaborate fantasies, but I challenge you to look at any world religion and not say the same of its prophets, saints, and gurus. When humans play in the realm of the sacred, we allow rationale to fall away in such wonderful ways. In fact, I would venture to say that the purpose of the sacred is to free us from the terrible confines of logic.

So, let's get on to contemporary history...

First, I take you back to the 1940s, the common starting era of three budding religions: Thelema, Wicca, and Scientology.

Egyptomania, along with images of Gods and Goddesses like Horus and Isis and historical figures like Cleopatra, were prevalent around the turn of the 20th century. However, a deep dive into brand new religions exploring Goddess figures gained a lot of momentum around the time of World War 2. The 40s and 50s are often viewed as very conservative times, but there was a very colorful and active counterculture, especially when it came to the occult.

The Scarlet Woman

We begin with the story of Scientology founder L. Ron Hubbard. He was staying at the home of rocket scientist Jack Parsons, and Jack's girlfriend Betty decided that she was more attracted to Hubbard. Jack was cool with it, but to work out his feelings of jealousy, he wanted to conjure up a female magical partner - an elemental. Parsons was a member of the order of Thelema, established at the turn of the century by Aleister Crowley. According to Parsons, the Red Goddess Babalon was the mother of all gods, a force that reconstructs a fallen world anew. She is the universal Feminine principle, and she takes residence on Earth as the Scarlet Woman.

Parsons called his mission The Babalon Working. He planned to cause the Goddess Babalon to embody a human form. And first, he needed his sex magic partner. A powerful fire element. After doing a number of rituals with Hubbard, which apparently involved plenty of blood and semen, strange things began happening. Lightning storms crashed through each night, and Hubbard said a mysterious ethereal force grabbed him. A few days later, Parsons, while out with Hubbard, suddenly proclaimed, "It is done." When he got back home, a woman was waiting there for them, brought by a friend who was dying to introduce her to Jack.

Her hair was fiery red, and she had intense blue eyes. She was the artist Marjorie Cameron, and she was an unusually witchy woman. Parsons knew it immediately. Cameron *was* the Scarlet Woman whom he had drawn to him.

The two hit it off and almost immediately began doing sex magic to conjure up the rebirth of Babalon. Cameron, as she preferred to be called, was an independent spirit though and left to study art in New York, where she had an abortion, not knowing that she and Parson's child was supposed to be born a deity. She traveled the world and came back to Parsons now and then. The two got married. Parsons had been one of the founders of the Jet Propulsion Laboratory, which was instrumental in getting NASA into space, but he was ousted when his involvement with Thelema was revealed. As the couple began to tire of one another, Cameron took a trip to Mexico and returned invigorated. She was planning to move there with Parsons, but right before they left for the trip the unthinkable happened. Jack was creating special effects explosives for a movie set, and he blew himself up in his home lab.

After Jack's death, Cameron went into a bit of a spiritual emergency. Even the members of Thelema thought she had lost her mind and ordered her excommunicated, and Crowley no longer took Parson's magical workings very seriously. But Cameron had found her husband's journals and began to fully appreciate her role in the process of raising Babalon.

In *Freedom is a Two-Edged Sword*, Jack wrote an enchantingly poetic chapter mocking patriarchal men and venerating women as the saviors of the human race. It begins:

> *"It is to you, woman, beautiful lost redeemer of the race, that I dare address this chapter. That which stirs in you now is not mad ness, is not sin, is not folly, but is life, new life, and joy and fire that will beget a new race, and create a new heaven and a new earth.*

When you were a child, did not the wind speak to you and the sun? Did you not hear the mountain's voice, the voices of the river and the storm? Have you not heard the tidings of the stars, and the voices in the silence, ineffable?

Have you not gone naked in the forest, with the wind over your body, and felt the caress of Pan? And your heart has swelled with spring, blossomed with summer, and saddened with the wolf of winter. These things are the covenant, and in them is the truth that is forever."

Cameron dated a black musician named Leroy Booth, and at that time in 1952, interracial relationships were still illegal. She enjoyed a lot of hallucinogens and ended up squatting in a house where she hosted lots of parties. She founded a sex magic cult of her own called The Children, which was deliberately mixed race. She planned to create a new family of what she called "moonchildren."

She was an admired artist but didn't often do gallery shows. In her first show, the 1957 exhibition at Los Angeles' Feris Gallery, was raided by the police and shut down for indecency because of her erotic drawing called *Peyote Vision*. It depicted a curvy nude woman on all fours, head thrown back in pleasure, with a serpentine tongue flicking from between her lips. Entering her from behind is a muscular figure with a peyote button in place of a head.

Cameron appeared as the Scarlet Woman in Kenneth Anger's Thelema-themed film *Inauguration of the Pleasure Dome*, alongside author Anais Nin. Nin was supposed to play the part, but Cameron told Anger, "I AM the Scarlet Woman." He could not help but agree.

She was a beloved figure on the L.A. art scene, and her work really stood out. To make a long story short (because I could write an entire book on Cameron alone.), she was known to have said things to her friends like, "Don't you know who I am?! I am Babalon!" She felt that Babalon had entered her during her rites with Parsons, and she was one and the same. Therefore, I count her as one of our first known Living Goddess figures in the United States.

The Red Goddess

This story didn't end with Cameron's death in 1995, however. There are practitioners today who carry on Babalon's rituals in a decidedly sadomasochistic way. Author Peter Grey writes about his blood sacrifices to Babalon. When speaking about his ritual piercings of his nipples and genitals, he says:

> "Through the ritual the male body is no longer seen as a closed story and is instead a site of transformation. And as a heterosexual man working with the mysteries of Babalon, such blood offerings are a key to the pylon of her mysteries."

> "This is the male formula, which is death, and it is the practice of annihilation that men need, rather than clinging to the Victorian fallacy of the will, the vigilized sigil,

or whatever other phylacteries used to avoid facing the loss of the self in the beloved."

Peter Grey also brings up the practices taught by my own mentor Cleo Dubois and her late husband Fakir Musafar. They introduced a flesh-pulling technique and popularized hook suspension within the BDSM community as a sacred ritual. For Grey, it is done in devotion to Babalon with the purpose of destroying the ego and to be annihilated in the Goddess. His talk on "becoming no man" is included in the notes if you want to delve further into it, as is his book *The Red Goddess.*

Drawing Down the Moon

Alongside Thelema, another new religion was taking shape: Wicca. And Gerald Gardner, credited for bringing Witchcraft to the forefront after the anti-witchcraft laws were finally repealed in England in 1951 (before which it was punishable by death), was highly influenced by Thelema. In fact, Wicca was thought of by figures like Aleister Crowley as its milder sister. It was all part of a kind of religious renaissance in that era. So, when I joined a coven in the early 1990s, Wicca had made its way into the mainstream. And, as a budding kinkster, one thing that caught my attention on my own coven's altar was the ritual scourge, a symbol of discipline. At that time, Wicca was by far more well-known and more widely practiced, at least in my own circles, than the Crowley style of magic. And the book *Drawing Down the*

Moon by Margot Adler, first published in 1979, was required reading in my coven. Our Priestess wanted us well educated in our history.

In the book, Adler describes how feminists in the 1960s, who had been primarily politically motivated, found sisterhood and power in neo-pagan groups that worshiped the Goddesses. They not only pushed back against the patriarchal structure of the predominant religion in returning to the Goddess, but they discovered that witchcraft was intrinsically related to women's power. And they found the rejection of what men often called "irrational" (think tarot cards, and other intuitive arts) was actually a rejection of, and fear of, the Divine Feminine.

Feminist Sylvia Federici goes into more detail on how women were persecuted as witches in order to squash women's strong social influence in her book *Caliban and the Witch*.

> *"What has not been recognized is that the witch-hunt was one of the most important events in the development of capitalist society and the formation of the modern proletariat. For the unleashing of a campaign of terror against women, unmatched by any other persecution, weakened the resistance of the European peasantry to the assault launched against it by the gentry and the state, at a time when the peasant community was already disintegrating under the combined impact of land privatization, increased taxation, and the extension of state control over every*

aspect of social life. The witch-hunt deepened the divisions between women and men, teaching men to fear the power of women, and destroyed a universe of practices, beliefs, and social subjects whose existence was incompatible with the capitalist work discipline, thus redefining the main elements of social reproduction."

"[A]t the ideological level, there is a close correspondence between the degraded image of women forged by the demonologists and the image of femininity constructed by the contemporary debates on the 'nature of the sexes,' which canonized a stereotypical woman, weak in body and mind and biologically prone to evil, that effectively served to justify male control over women and the new patriarchal order."

Needless to say, witchcraft and the power and dominance of women are intimately related topics. And groups like one formed in 1968 called W.I.T.C.H., also known as Women's International Terrorist Conspiracy from Hell, knew this when performing curses and doing "zaps" (improvised hit-and-run guerilla theater) against patriarchal institutions. They invoked witchcraft as a power move.

At any rate, our history of Female Dominant Religion would not be complete without neo-pagan figures such as Z Budapest. Z was a proponent of matriarchy, a separatist, and the grandmother of Dianic witchcraft. Unfortunately, her politics took a hateful turn when she decided to exclude trans women from her Goddess Festival. I find her to be a cautionary tale: when we operate from fear rather than from power, all that was achieved before in power is tainted. The worry that men will find a way to take over our sacred spaces by pretending to be women is admittedly based in a heartfelt devotion to fighting for female dominance. But it's also misguided. It's a warning against mixing anxiety-filled bio-essentialism with spiritual concepts. You will begin to align with the dominant patriarchal religion steeped in fear. What I found most interesting, however, is how her actions conflicted with ideas she had put forth earlier in her work.

A quote from her: "Religion controls inner space; inner space controls outer space."

I agree with that quote wholeheartedly. Inner space does indeed control outer space, which makes her superficial focus on genitalia pretty surprising.

I felt as I read those words that I had to include her, as both a caution regarding a direction I *don't* think Female Dominant religion should go, but also as a figure who saw the important link between Female Dominance and religion. In her writing, she emphasized that if we could think of ourselves as Priestesses, and have the experience of embodying Goddesses, we would behave differently out in the world.

Some pagan groups, including the one I was a part of for many years, commonly practiced what is called "Drawing Down." In this practice, the Priestess is consecrated and draws whichever Goddess is invoked into her own body, often speaking as the Goddess herself. The Priestess becomes Goddess. And she is worshiped, and the devotees interact with her directly. She is Woman as temporary Deity.

Aristasia

However, let's take a slight detour from that train of thought. If some of you have a more monotheistic leanings, rather than seeing Woman as Deity, there are groups who see the one God as Feminine - as Mother God, which brings me to Aristasia. Those into lesbian BDSM lore might recognize the name, Miss Martindale.

In the 1970s, there was a commune in Donegal, Ireland, called Atlantis, known locally as "the Screamers." They were a Gestalt psychology group known mostly for the way they would go out into the yard and scream their heads off to release pent-up anger and mourning. Marianne Martindale, now known as Mary Guillermin (married to filmmaker Peter Guillermin, director of the 1976 King Kong movie in another weird little connection to the movie biz), took over the house that the commune occupied and, after the Gestalt screamers left, she turned it into the Silver Sisterhood. This was a Woman led group who worshiped God as Mother and said that everything they did was in reverence to Her. They didn't use electricity, wore long dresses and covered their hair, made crafts by hand, and grew their own food.

In 1984 that morphed into St. Brides, also known as Aristasia. Members wore elaborate anachronistic Victorian-style clothing, and still eschewed modernity. They also published their own magazines and books, which included scenes of paddling and spanking, and developed several CD-ROM video games. Their home was also, in part, a Victorian boarding school for "girls" (all adult women) where corporal punishment was the norm.

I have had a number of interesting correspondences with Mary, who is now a therapist in California and has done a one-woman theatrical show about her own spiritual journey. She was a little prickly about my interest in Aristasia's kinky practices.

In an email with me, she said, *"The only surrender I am interested in for myself and others is surrender to the divine will of the Mother-God and her Daughter -- cf. www.mother-god.com."* Later, as I continued to correspond with her about her religious interests, she said:

> *"I expect you can imagine how many emails I have received over the years about the illustrious Miss M. I do not disavow physical discipline as potentially spiritual and purifying -- although in a sense I have, because after all those years that we strayed towards the edge of "domination" (something we were never interested in despite appearances) in case there were female souls truly interested in the Mother, we had to rescind physical discipline altogether for ourselves as well -- the interest in Dea was never genuine and the interest in discipline was only about sexual gratification it turned out.*
>
> *There were words and phrases in your email that made you sound too interested in domination for my philosophy and sensibility."*

But regardless of her objection to the prurient nature of

my interest in her history, I was also quite interested in the religious materials she shared with me and took it upon myself to read her book *The Gospel of Our Mother God*. I was delighted to find she referenced Sanskrit texts in the book and particularly focused on the Padma Purana, a devotional hymn to Lakshmi. And this so nicely ties into my next group, and probably my favorite.

The Service of Mankind Church

The Service of Mankind Church began in 1979 and is still active today, and is, in fact, in the process of expanding. I've had the pleasure of getting to know the current high priestess, MaitresseX, and I'll be including one of their beautiful rituals in my film in progress called *Finding Love*.

A little more background from me: At the very young age of 18, I was put in charge of protecting the Tantra exhibit and the reconstruction of a Saiva temple inside the Nelson-Atkins Museum of Art in Kansas City. As a result of my quiet eight-hour days simply standing with the relics, strange things began to happen. I would enter trances that would create a kind of amnesia for hours at a time. It was as if in those trances, the entire blueprint of all that is was laid out before me. As I came out of that space, I would have spontaneous orgasms. I was in the midst of an experience I have only begun to explain.

After that, I found myself spontaneously wandering into devotional rituals, called pujas, in unlikely places. At a nudist colony in California, I was drawn in by the sound of drums and chanting. While shopping at a high-end Chicago antique store, the salesmen took me for a ride in the service elevator. I was led through the gallery to a large stone doorway, beyond which I found myself pouring a ladle of water over a large and elaborately decorated Shiva Lingam. There are hidden temples everywhere, and I seemed to stumble into them again and again.

So, I began to study Hinduism. First, academically, studying Hindu Art in grad school and taking classes on history and religion through Oxford's Hindu Studies program. My interest became less and less academic, and I eventually joined an ashram for a couple of years and studied a bit of Sanskrit. In my late 30s, when I was running a BDSM dungeon in Chicago, I really began to think about the religious potential of Female Domination in terms of honoring the Goddess Kali. The image of Kali standing on Shiva was a source of endless fascination for me (and sometimes a source of fear and confusion for my Indian sex work clientele who didn't expect to see her in that context). Somehow, in researching the idea, I came upon the Essemian Manifesto. The copy I have was published in 1983. Prominent in the publication were images of Kali standing on Shiva.

I knew I found my people. But as far as I knew, they were no longer a group. They were mysterious. Their simple website never changed from the 1990s. Recently, however, I was introduced to them through our mutual friend Sylvie during Sylvie's quest to record the history of FemDom, and it all came together! They are still an ongoing religion. Finally, Goddess worship and BDSM are explicitly linked as part of a fully-fledged legal church. It is drawing down; it is Female

Domination; it is a physical discipline, bondage, sadomasochism, and religious ecstasy - everything rolled into one.

About Kali, the Manifesto quotes a book called *Sexual Secrets, The Alchemy of Ecstasy*:

> *"A woman becomes one with Kali by coming to terms with her own awesome power of initiation. As an initiatress into the sexual mysteries of Kali, woman is the ultimate guru of man."*

The ideas of controlled suffering in the Essemian manifesto echo the blood rites of Babalon for stripping the man of his ego. The Manifesto quotes Dr. Lynn Cowan from her book on Masochism:

> *"Masochistic reduction of the ego, to basics, to shadow, to body, is a baseline experience. It seems to be a necessary process - less, perhaps, for sexual pleasure than for humus of psychic earth, for the very health and vitality of the soul."*

She goes on to write about the ego becoming a servant to a "greater thing," which may be called Goddess in the case of Female Domination.

For those interested in the SMC, they have a meetup group and are starting to become more active online once again, and I've included their information in the notes.

Guru Rasa

Also emerging in the 1980s was the fascinating figure of the Guru Rasa von Werder. Her name is Kellie Everts, and she appeared regularly on daytime TV talk shows. First as a celibate stripper for God, and later as a Dominatrix with a following of religious devotees. In a 1988 clip of Kellie as she appeared on the *Morton Downey, Jr. Show*, she and the host aggressively bump chests in a standoff between female supremacy and male chauvinism.

Guru Rasa published a number of books, including essays by her devotees, and is best known for *Woman, Thou Art God*, in which she says that men are attracted to the beauty of the female form because of their longing for Mother God. Her group, the University of MotherGod Church, like Aristasia, is monotheistic. She views herself as an Avatar of God - here on earth to help others get closer to the divine through sacred sexuality. Kellie has a YouTube channel where she talks about her entire history in sex work and as a figure of worship and devotion (see notes).

The Cybelian Order

With the help of MaitresseX of the SMC, I also found information on another FemDom group called the Cybelian Movement. They are named after the great Goddess Cybele, whose worship rivaled that of Isis around the 200s BCE. The Cybelian Order of today started in 2004. They have members in 100 different countries and have their own unique set of rituals. One of the key pillars of their movement includes the regular use of the male submissive as a toilet. The stated purpose of the Cybelian Order is to empower women to become assertive in their marriages. And as such, the woman is in full control of her sexuality, and cuckolding is the norm.

In Cybelian marriage ceremonies, all are dressed except for the groom, who is totally nude and collared. The groomsmen all have sex with the bride in front of him, and then she urinates on him, and the wedding guests are invited to do the same. It's undoubtedly a very kinky ceremony and group! I have included a link to the Cybelians website in the notes.

The U.G.R.

And finally, a while back, I was invited to become a part of an entire micronation called the Universal Gynecocratic Republic. I am still unsure how many citizens are part of this Republic, which is decidedly female supremacist in nature and has its own currency, which only women are allowed to hold. In fact, men have no rights as citizens and serve women completely. It's a fairly simple process to become a citizen, at least as a woman. And I'm also unsure of how many people meet and practice their ideology and rituals as a group, and how much of it is just a fantasy of an alternative society - a femocratic utopia of sorts. So they kind of skirt by my criteria for being verifiable as a real-life organization, though the founders live in Eastern Europe and have told me they live the lifestyle they described on their website 24/7. I decided to include them because of the descriptions of their unique religious practice, which seems to be an important part of their community.

Their central Goddess is Venus, and their mythology includes Lilith as the daughter of Venus who created the universe. The biblical figure of Adam is the antagonist in their religious mythology, and Lilith must save Eve from his domination and reclaim paradise. The eight-pointed Venus Star is their symbol. Women may move from Venrea to Priestess with eight years of training, in coordination with the eight-pointed star.

The Moon is also central to their religious rites. It is said to be how Venus communicates with her followers, and women-only full moon rituals are held monthly. They say they hold "games" in honor of Venus every two years where men are used as chariots and put through a number of other kinky ordeals from strap-on races to ball-busting competitions. Frankly, it sounds like a whole lot of kinky fun!

I did, however, fall into an argument with the founders of the U.G.R. over raising children in Gynarchy. At the time I wrote this, they seem to have been advocating the abuse of young boys by girls, as well as chastity for males as soon as they enter puberty.

This only returns us to the patriarchy-in-reverse paradigm. In my view, that is still not Gynarchy. To maintain emotionally healthy Hives, we must be aware of age-appropriate education. It's important that kids are educated on the body and the basics of sexuality, but beyond that, children are unable to consent to participating in or witnessing sexual and kink activities with adults.

And I mentioned this in my previous book, *150 Years of Gynarchy*, though the underlying power dynamics of

Gynarchy will be obvious to the children we raise, the goal is not to make boys feel worthless or turn girls into mini dominatrices, but to simply model fulfilling roles for men and women. Our first pillars are Consent and Bodily Autonomy. As I pointed out in the psychology chapter, these apply to everyone and are especially important for children.

Call to Action

And so we've followed the journey of the history of contemporary FemDom religion from Babalon to Kali to Cybele to Lilith with lots of sacred kink and D/s and sex magic mixed in as integral parts of the rites and practices. And it's all led by women as Goddesses and women as Priestesses and Gurus of their own unique cults.

With that, I say unto you, the possibility to become a Living Goddess, and not just roleplay as one, is there for you if you choose to embody the Feminine Divine. If you are called to take this seriously and dare. Let us give ourselves permission. There is nothing stopping you. Let us create temples and install ourselves at the center as Dominant Women, as gurus, as Priestesses, as literal Goddesses, according to our own vision of spirituality. Ensure women's freedom and bodily autonomy as part of your basic tenants. Incorporate devotion and worship to open the heart.

Do not mistake worship for pumping up your ego. Allowing another person to be able to show devotion is a great gift *to them*. Devotion is powerful medicine. It creates ecstasy in the devotee and can heal the wounds of the individual and the world. In the Saiva tradition, there are words for these things: Seva - selfless service; and Bhakti - devotion. These are long-known paths to enlightenment. Even in monotheism, the very act of devotion brings you closer to the divine.

And none of us needs to achieve some status of fully enlightened being in order to help one another on this path of evolution toward divinity. The secrets are inside every one of us, and we only need each other to uncover them.

Incorporate your skills in sadomasochism to open the body in the ways described in Sacred Kink and use humiliation, and selfless service for men to surpass their ego and find their true nature. Let's create a network of Goddesses across the globe, the density of which steals the very oxygen away from patriarchy and just may, in turn, save our lovely planet.

In my work with my own worldwide organization, I have found that women are open and willing to work together without competition toward the common goal of increasing our collective power in society. Religion is an incredibly useful tool in doing so, and we should use it to our full advantage. It doesn't have to be deathly serious. The nature of reality is playful. It's fluid and bends to our delight. It is in play that we understand the workings of the universe. Let us be ecstatic in our play with power.

Women should take up more space in religion as both fully human and fully divine. We can make the rules, and design a community, a network, and by extension, a world that we want to live in.

PART 4

THE DEVI DOCTRINE

The new and ancient religion of Gynarchy

I want to know my God
At least enough to fear Her
If I can't be the song
At least have mercy, let me hear Her
    Sevdaliza, *Eden*

A note on the appropriation of language.

The Devi Doctrine incorporates a lot of words in the Sanskrit language to talk about various ideas and practices. There may be some who voice an objection to this and consider it cultural appropriation. However, almost every religion today is universal, and its adherents use the ancient languages of their religions regardless of where they live. New Muslims in America use the word Allah for their god and speak the Shahada in Arabic in order to convert. Studied Taoists in the West still use Chinese terms like "wu wei" because the English translations seem insufficient or too wordy. Jewish converts use phrases in Hebrew like Shabbat and Shalom, and Western Buddhists use words like Maya and Dharma, which are also Sanskrit terms. It might also be interesting to note that most Indians and Hindus no longer speak Sanskrit and scholars work hard to preserve it as well as the essential ancient texts written in it. So, though it comes from Indian culture, less than 25,000 in India speak Sanskrit as their mother tongue.

Many concepts herein originate within traditions first recorded in the Sanskrit language. They are important and relevant concepts. I could use not-quite-equivalent English terms or make up new words for these very old ideas, but it seems more respectful to maintain them in their original form and allow their meanings to resonate through their sounds. Because everything is sound.

| 4-1 |

Para Vidya

Higher Knowledge

1 Devi

All known creation is vibration. Nada Brahma - all is sound. Devi is the vibration of creation from which all matter, energy, thought, feeling, sensation, and movement is formed. She is The Mother of All, the life force that shapes us, animates us, and gives us conscious awareness.

Throughout time, all human cultures have known of The Mother, though some have forgotten. That Mother is the symbolic expression of Devi. She has many forms and many names and is embodied in many places at once, in stone and bronze, in art, in nature, and in flesh. Each aspect of her, new and old, is a unique expression to be worshiped as a deity.

In the state of the silent, still, undefined, and absolute potential She is Siva - literally "that which is not." We can immerse ourselves in this infinite and boundless state through meditation, trance, or death. It is our built-in reset program which rescues our minds and nervous systems from chaos and overstimulation. The more practiced we become the more we can carry the boundlessness, peace, and silence with us into everyday life.

2 Desire

Desire To Be is the cause and motivation of all existence. It is that which caused the differentiation between "that which is" and "that which is not."

Desire to Know - to answer the question "What am I?"- created a third state, making all of the infinite iterations of creation possible. It allowed for the threefold division of knower, knowing, and known to materialize, and made variations of thought, form, and movement erupt into being. Every facet and every detail is its own piece of information meant to answer Devi's question "What am I?" She answers Herself: "I am this, and I am this, and I am this, and I am this..."

The Desire to Know in humans activates within us to show us the nature of existence. All self-conscious beings possess the Desire to Know. The Desire to Know is symbolized in the form of the serpent, who sleeps coiled within and is awakened.

3 Lila (Play)

All that lives and exists in the universe is the infinite creative play of Devi, meant to be marveled at and enjoyed to the fullest. Don't be fooled. Even that which appears serious or grim is just part of Her game. And therefore, there is never need for fear and anxiety.

The opposite of fear is Love. Love is taking the concerns of the other as your own. Love of Devi is identifying with and surrendering to Devi so as to know Her. That Love negates and neutralizes fear.

Our ultimate purpose as humans is to be a channel for Devi's Desires. We are mechanisms by which She creates and expands. If we can sit quietly and listen, allowing logic and reason to fall away, the subtle vibrations of all Her emerging Desires will move through us effortlessly and become clear.

Her Desires come through us in actions and expressions of self which are authentic, and through our unique and autonomous perspectives. Resisting or blocking the flow of Her Desire creates inevitable challenges and dams up creativity.

Devi's essential qualities are: creative, abundant, cyclical, playful, active, attractive, and sensual. All objects, actions, or energies that may stifle or pervert these qualities are simple obstacles which prevent us from being fully attuned to Devi. Look to the Dark Feminine to find and remove the obstacles.

4 The Trellis and the Flowering Vine

Devi, the Divine Feminine, has no equal or opposite. She created the divine masculine for a purpose.

First, he is the trellis to Her flowering vine. Without the trellis, the vine will still grow, but with it, the vine takes new shapes and directions and thrives, reaching ever toward the light. Without the trellis, the vine is more vulnerable to that which can harm it and its fruits might lay on the ground and decay.

The trellis alone without the vine stands with no purpose, upright and casting a long shadow, but easier to blow over without the weight of the vine wrapped around it. It is a scaffolding without a use. Structural and stoic, without lush beauty and growth.

Because he gives her snaking tendrils the lines and angles on which to hold, he plays a second role. He is her witness and scribe, the translator of metaphor into math, of symbol into words. He finds underlying logic in Her patterns and rhythm in Her pulses and waves.

He remembers. He creates shorthand. He stores memory in bits, encoded as ones and zeros so She can easily call up lost passwords and combinations. She is raw data and he is the formula that describes and organizes it.

5 Woman and Man

Likewise, Devi created Woman to populate the Earth and be an agent of Her Desire. She engendered the Desire to Know coiled within Her, and Consciousness of Self and Awareness of Others in order that she might play, engage, enjoy, and ponder all of creation.

Woman, too, is a creator. She is Devi of the flesh. When she forgets this, or when her power is bound too tightly or oppressed, She suffers.

Thereafter Devi created man from the body of Woman and in the image of Woman, as an expression of the divine masculine, to lend variety and stability to Woman. The genes he contributes to the creation of other humans act as a protection against disease.

Man was created to support and love Her, and to be the enchanted witness to creation and describe, count, and catalog all that he sees.

He is the tooth of the serpent - he who is shaped by the Desire to Know, but who, without Love of Devi, becomes a lost fragment, not privy to the bigger picture.

6 The Devi and the dasa

The Living Goddess is the embodiment of the Divine Feminine. The center of Her spiritual Hive. She fully acknowledges that She is Devi Herself in differentiated and consecrated form, as a human Woman. She is both fully human and fully divine.

She has made herself a clear and open conduit for Devi's Desire, while at the same time maintaining a perspective unique to her place in time and context.

Her many human faults make her a deity that one can see, hear, touch, and relate to. Without them, she would be made of stone. But at times she will seem distant and will need long periods of quiet meditation to remain grounded in everyday reality while being ever attuned to Desire.

The dasa is the ultimate expression of the divine masculine. He is supportive in every way, facilitating ease and flow, adding stability, order, and security to the life of his Living Goddess.

He is a witness to Her, fully and deeply aware of Her divinity, paying careful attention and recording both Her Desires and Her acts of creation. More than an average devotee, he has made Her his life's focus.

In turn, She has opened his heart wide, tamed his ego, and led him to better understand the nature of his existence and his reason for being. He is fully able to take on her concerns as if they were his own, and he will take on any task or any role in order to bring her pleasure and joy.

He is sometimes the messenger between the Living Goddess and others, a protective layer to keep her annoyances and distractions to a minimum.

7 Laboratory Earth

The universe which sprang from Devi has in it a laboratory, a sandbox within which contrasts and compliments are mixed and matched in endless experimental glee. The laboratory is Earth, and there is nothing in the universe like it, with the conditions made just right for the ripening of Desire in three dimensions.

The lab is sealed off to maintain the integrity of the experiment, and the dimensions beyond its doors can scarcely be imagined by the humans within. Though self-aware they are sealed in, with only the device of the mind to probe limits beyond their senses.

That is until the Desire to Know uncoils, fully awake within them, to give them a different kind of sight.

| 4 - 2 |

The Purpose

Here

The point and purpose of living is to experience and enjoy the awe-inspiring variety and complexity of Devi's ongoing and endless creation.

In doing so, you are able to love Devi, be a conduit and tool of Her Desires, and realize unity with Her in a very real way. This eliminates fear and anxiety.

When in love with Devi, the vibration that makes up your being, consciousness and body are tuned to be in complete harmony with everything around you. You experience a feeling of connection to all. Conflicts fall away, and your intelligence, awareness, and empathy increase. Creativity, abundance, and ease envelop you.

This is not a difficult path if you are able to simply remember. Remember the Mother.

Devi consciousness uncoils the serpent within, and the Desire to Know fully awakens. You gain knowledge of what moves beyond the laboratory Earth. You gain an understanding of the bigger picture, which cannot be described in the language of words.

Hereafter

Devi Doctrine doesn't teach a concept of an afterlife, nor heaven or hell. In death, like a drop of water in a vast ocean, "that which is you" returns to merge into Siva - "that which is not." Reincarnation exists only in the fact that every bit of energy that is created gets cycled and recycled into something new. The energy which animates you and gives you conscious awareness is no different.

You are but a mechanism, or a program, designed to gain a unique perspective on the answer to Devi's question "What am I?"

The goal in this life becomes orchestrating a connected existence of exuberance and fearless exploration while learning to understand what you are, as well as what lies beyond the senses. There are mysteries unspoken.

Energetic and emotional echoes and reverberations of your unique presence remain on Earth forever, as well as any acts of creation you contributed to the planet, be they knowledge, art, or human offspring. What echoes and traces will you leave behind?

| 4-3 |

Bhakti

Actions/Behaviors of the Devotee

The Devi Doctrine is primarily a path of devotion or "Bhakti." But action, knowledge, and direct experience play significant roles. The Bhakti path removes arrogance, jealousy, anger, hatred, and egoism and replaces them with divine ecstasy, bliss, and wisdom.

The Devi devotee seeks to open the heart and release fear and open the eyes and see what is real. Being given a point of focus, someone to whom they can surrender - a Living Goddess in which to pour their love and service - is a true gift to a devotee. It clears the path, smooths the road, and puts them on a fast track to a fulfilled existence.

When you find your Living Goddess, you know. You are filled with something akin to obsession. It is called Cathexis. Cathexis is a prerequisite to falling in love. Cathexis is the heart-opening process and love is the result. Cathexis is the feeling that makes you keep the Living Goddess foremost in your thoughts because you cannot help otherwise. It focuses life energy in a singular direction, like the inner compass pointing true North. It sets the stage for devotion.

You may dream of Her. You may hear Her voice in your head when you are alone. Your thoughts always return to Her. These are signs that she is your Living Goddess, and you should approach and offer your devotion and service.

A devotee who has committed fully may earn the honor of being called "dasa" by their Living Goddess. It means servant of the deity, or one who has surrendered to the deity. It has been translated as "slave" though it has nothing to do with non-consensual chattel slavery.

The 4 Internal Challenges

As the devotee steps onto the path, however, they may face challenges within them which create a detour or pause their journey. These are quite normal and can be overcome.

The Challenge of Impatience

When one finds their Goddess it can lead to a feeling of frenzy. You want to do everything. You want to know everything about Her. And you need it all to happen right now. Your only want is to be always in Her presence or in constant contact and absorb all you can. Enjoy the feeling, but do not allow yourself to become agitated and impatient when things don't move as quickly or as intensely as you would like. Your Goddess may first deliberately test your patience before offering up any other lessons. Allow the frenzy to settle into a steady, easy hum that propels you through your day.

The Challenge of Entitlement

If stuck in a transactional mindset, one might feel that when one is doing so many things to please and serve the Goddess, one must be entitled to some small thing in return. That something could be Her time and attention, words of praise, a smile, acknowledgment, favored treatment, or a quick response to one's email. It is this sense of entitlement that creates uncomfortable feelings of resentment, not the Goddess Herself. Her only obligation is to allow you to view Her as an object of veneration and graciously accept the love you pour into Her, that your heart may open and your ego lay down in obedience when in Her presence.

The Challenge of Centering

To adjust to the Bhakti path, you must begin to pay close attention to where you center your perspective. You may be surprised at how often you view yourself as the main character in the whole universe's story. How often can you catch yourself recognizing that you've centered your wants, your needs, your values, your expectations, and your point of view? The Goddess provides you the opportunity to grow your empathy ten thousandfold. And you do this by simply re-centering your perspective with Her as the central character. It takes careful study but try to begin to see everything from the perspective of Her values, wants, needs, vision, and point of view. You will find your mind expanded.

The Challenge of Ennui

One must face the fact that often being a devotee can be tedious. You may be asked to engage in repetitive routines and rituals. You may have to do tasks and drudgework that is not particularly stimulating. Don't let boredom set you off course. If you forget that each and every action is an act of love and devotion, you may begin to moan, whine and complain. In doing so, you tell your Goddess that what she wants from you is unimportant and that Her wishes are putting you out when you could be doing so many more fun and interesting things. Instead, focus on doing everything well and with conscious intention, even waiting for your next instructions.

The Remedies

There are certain disciplines and practices that are key to gaining the sense of closeness and unity that you desire with your Goddess. They are remedies to your inevitable internal challenges that remind you of your place and your purpose.

Nandi

The concept of Nandi is named after the bull Vahana (mount, or vehicle) belonging to Shiva, the Adi Yogi (that means original yogi, in contrast to Siva, which is the broader concept of "that which is not."). He is meant to show devotees the proper attitude.

Shiva was known to go into deep meditation for very long periods of time - possibly thousands of years. Nandi, his bull, would sit waiting for him, a contented look on his face, resting, with one hoof raised and ready to stand at any moment.

His waiting was not passive. He was not sleeping. It was an active, aware, and alert kind of waiting. If Shiva changed his facial expression, Nandi would notice. He was ready to spring into action and be of service whenever needed. The contented look on his face showed that he was willing to wait forever without complaint. To overcome impatience and ennui, practice being like the bull Nandi. Challenge yourself to ever-extended times of sitting in alert patience or mantra meditation without falling asleep.

Seva

Seva means selfless service. This is not service done to make yourself feel righteous for having been such a good and kind person. It is done without any motives other than the act of service itself. It is utterly empty of transactional thought or expectations. It's not done for personal gain or to gain favor or gratitude from others. It is plainly motivated by the wish to serve. It helps to get ego out of your way and to increase empathy and attunement to the needs of others. To practice selfless service, you only ask what needs to be done, and do it. In doing so, you may feel a strange sense of immeasurable joy, which may become addictive. But don't go in with that feeling as your end goal. Approach it as a service for the sake of service alone. It is also important that you not use it to judge and compete with others, comparing notes on who serves more. This is a great remedy to decenter yourself and remove feelings of entitlement. It also keeps you from getting bored and occupies your time so you can avoid impatience.

Puja

Puja is a daily ritual of devotion. The devotee keeps an altar and sits before it in communion with his Goddess (or Goddesses). Usually, there will be an image of Her at the center, or a symbol representing Her. First, he will cleanse his body. He will bow deeply in reverence to her image and strike or ring a bell or gong. Then he will offer the elements (incense as air, lamp or candle as fire, water, and salt or something of substance grown in earth, as well as an oil to represent ether) and other gifts such as flowers, coins, perfume, fruits, sweets, etc. The gifts should be significant to his individual Goddess. This is followed by Her favorite mantras, reciting Her name 108 times, and/or a pledge to the Goddess which She has written for this purpose. Only if instructed by Her, he may engage in self-flagellation to remind him to remain disciplined, or masturbation (without orgasm) to raise erotic energy as an offering to Her. And, if there is time, this is followed by a period of meditation and/or contemplation on the Goddess. He will end the puja with another deep bow or by laying his body prostrate on the floor to position himself as low as possible before her image, and a final ringing of the bell. Puja is a beautiful reminder of your place and purpose and will ease the frenzied or agitated mind.

Darshan

Darshan is looking upon or making visual contact with the deity or holy person. In person, Darshan can often involve a lesson given by the Goddess, or a discussion where She answers questions. The devotee will sit at her feet and gaze upon her intently. If he is lucky, She will make eye contact, which is a powerful form of blessing, personally acknowledging the love and service of the devotee. Some Goddesses will allow the devotee or devotees to bow and kiss, anoint, or worship Her feet. It is the direct interaction between devotee and Deity. But Darshan need not be in person. One may receive Darshan by simply gazing upon an image - a photo or drawing - of his Goddess, looking deeply into Her eyes. It is often enough to bring about incredible feelings of love and an altered state of consciousness for the devotee. And doing so while also hearing a recording of Her voice can feel no different than if She were there in person. In some more powerful instances of Darshan, the devotee may feel compelled to cry, laugh, dance, moan, or even flail on the floor in ecstasy. He may feel he has been shot into outer space. This is a powerful remedy to decenter the self, and will cure any sense of mental agitation, fear, or ennui.

The Five Steps

Symbolized as the five circling petals of the hibiscus flower, there are five steps the devotee takes upon entering the service of a Living Goddess. They are taken in order.

Surrender

The first step is necessary before any of the others. This is the realization that you truly want your life to be led by the Living Goddess. You sincerely have no wish to be in control. In trust, with open eyes and an open heart, you let go of fear and surrender to Her Desire.

Submit

Yield to Her authority and put up no resistance. You say yes. You learn to know Her. Your ego lies down quietly at Her feet and you obey Her.

Sacrifice

Sacrifice things that once felt important but no longer have meaning or do not serve you on your path. Superficial attachments dissolve. For Her, you can release what needs to be released. You realize the insignificance of minor matters that once loomed large.

Serve

Be of practical use in making Her life better, easier, and more pleasurable. Find pleasure in your ability to be useful and competent and take on every task as an act of love. Serve without expectation.

Survive

This is both the survival of human life on Earth renewed by our devotion to the Feminine, and the survival of your spiritual commitment to Devi. You persist and endure, your steps steady and assured.

Actions/Behaviors of the Living Goddess

Embodying Love

A Living Goddess must be able to allow people to love Her. This may be harder than it sounds. It is an active process of attracting and drawing out love from another, cleaving their heart wide open. It is allowing Her power as the embodiment of love itself to flow freely through Her and reach out and pull others in seemingly effortlessly, like a vortex. It means being unperturbed and unafraid when someone falls to Her feet and proclaims that he is Hers. She must fall in love freely and often whenever She sees someone's heart. She is capable of experiencing all flavors of love. But She must also be able to sit firm in Her own power of Desire, not allowing the desires of others to sway Her away from Her own. Her Desire is the ultimate guide. It is the Desire of Devi moving through Her. She has the unique privilege and responsibility of being the catalyst for Her devotees' spiritual evolution, and the focus of their efforts.

Devi's Desire

A Living Goddess is an agent of Devi's Desire. Devi's Desire is not an immutable proclamation from on high; not the "will of the gods" unfathomable and imposing. For the Living Goddess, to know Devi's Desire is to simply sit with the question "What do I want?" And it may begin very small. "I want a drink of water." But as the Living Goddess becomes more practiced at asking, She will find the larger answers which resonate like the strike of a gong through her entire being. It is not an analytical process of reasoning and guessing what She wants. She allows the answers to come to Her and checks them for authenticity. "Is this what I want?" What She wants will move Her. The answers for every Living Goddess will be different because She is a unique expression of Devi. But if answers align among Goddesses, a broader Desire is being expressed.

Consecration

Consecration of the Living Goddess can happen in many ways. It may happen through Her own long and steady Sadhana (spiritual practice: meditation, trance, puja, etc.) that She comes to the moment when She realizes Her readiness. It may happen without warning, like a bolt out of the blue, that She enters a trance, sees the design of existence laid out before Her, and instantly knows Her role in it. This is spontaneous Shaktipat (a transference of spiritual experience or awareness) from Devi Herself. She may also be consecrated by another Living Goddess, receiving Shaktipat from Her, and may even be mentored in creating Her Temple and Hive. Consecration is the alchemical process of becoming holy and sacred, of becoming fully conscious of the self as Divine; of the self as Devi. It is common for devotees to refer to a consecrated Woman simply as Devi or Devi followed by her first name.

Every Woman has the innate potential to be realized as a Living Goddess; a few are born wielding this power from day one. Not every woman will want to be consecrated as a Living Goddess, as she has a different path to take and different concerns, and she does not wish to take on the responsibility of becoming the central focus of the devotion of many. However, obstacles to a Woman's wish to be consecrated might be issues of ego. Either she has become mired in the perverse feminine and wants to be worshiped out of the need to feel important and to use her power over others to assuage her feelings of insecurity, or her insecurity and lack of self-knowledge make her feel unworthy. The motivation to become a Living Goddess will emerge from a sincere wish to serve and lead others and from a profound understanding of Devi's Desire.

The Holy Humanness of the Goddess

It is important for the Living Goddess to maintain Her humanity. She should show Her devotees that she feels the full spectrum of human emotion and is capable of real empathy. She should eat, breathe, shit, and orgasm as a Woman, and enjoy all aspects of Her human existence. She is still a one-of-a-kind participant in the infinite multiplicity and diversity of the planet. Her intuition will be heightened and Her perspective on all of existence broadened, but her body of flesh and blood is still crucial in Her role. She may be more inclined to live a healthy lifestyle, but she can suffer illness and injury just as Her devotees suffer.

There are no hard and fast protocols on how a Living Goddess must speak or behave. Each is marvelously unique. Her purpose is to attract specific devotees who can attune to Her Desires and who wish to have a living human Woman onto which to focus their feelings of love, devotion, and service. Divine love becomes a fully embodied experience of Divinity, not an abstract one. Humans can begin their spiritual evolution through the worship of a statue of stone or bronze. However, Women are the natural embodiment of love for human beings, beginning with our first feelings for our mothers when we are infants. It is a path more comforting and familiar for most.

There will be times a Living Goddess begins to lose Her human inclinations. When this happens, She will dive deep into extended meditation, lasting days or weeks. During these times She is exploring and expanding, gaining new wisdom, tracing new energetic channels between Her and devotees or other Goddesses, or recharging Herself to emerge again with greater energy. Or She may be preparing to leave. A Goddess of very old age or experiencing terminal illness will eventually stop communicating with devotees directly. She will spend more and more time in meditation, resting on the subtle edge of "that which is not." It is best not to disturb Her during these times, but to carry on with your devotions.

| 4-4 |

Sacred Practices and Rites

Along with the essential concepts of Nandi, Seva, Puja, and Darshan, there are many other rites and practices that may be a part of life in a Gynarchic Hive. Each Living Goddess should keep Her own private Book of Rites with more detailed instructions for carrying out sacraments, ceremonies, and rituals. These are best not made public in order to protect the sanctity of each Hive's religious system. But within the congenial Gynarchy network, the Goddess may reach out to gain knowledge from other Living Goddesses. Her own knowledge and Her Desires will shape the spiritual culture of Her hive. There will be practices that are specific to each Hive, but most will participate in at least some version of the following:

Meditation

Mantra meditation is effective at bringing the practitioner closer and closer to the most subtle vibration of existence, thereby allowing them to reset their nervous system and bring the peace of Siva out into their everyday life. Mantras should only be given to the meditator by their Goddess and will be a bija or "seed" mantra (or a string of seed mantras). These are words in Sanskrit chosen for the specific power of the vibration of their sounds. It is best to keep the mantra secret between the meditator and their Goddess, and not share it with others. During the initial meditation, the mantra is first repeated out loud. It is repeated in progressively quieter tones until it is barely audible. It is then repeated only within the mind, silently. After the first meditation, it never needs to be spoken out loud again except at the request of a Goddess.

Sitting comfortably with the eyes closed, and breathing normally, the meditator repeats the mantra mentally for 21 minutes, allowing all thoughts to come and go without trying to direct them or force them away. If the meditator gets lost in thought, they should gently return to the repetition of the mantra. It should feel effortless. At the end of 21 minutes, the meditator stops the repetition, sits with eyes closed for one to two minutes, and then gently comes back to their normal waking state. The point of the meditation is to occupy the space between waking and sleep for long periods, which causes brainwave coherence and a total refresh of the entire nervous system. If possible, this should be done twice daily, in the morning and late afternoon or evening.

Cyclical Rites

Full and New Moon Rituals

The Divine Feminine is cyclical. And our calendars used to be kept by looking at the moon. The full moon is a time when energies are at their peak and about to subside, and it is a good time for letting go of what no longer serves you. The new moon is the best time to state intentions and begin new endeavors, using the pull of the waxing moon to add momentum. The new moon is also an excellent time to engage in dream rituals as the lack of reflected sunlight means sleep is deeper and less disturbed.

Solstice and Equinox Celebrations

The Solstices are when we experience the longest and shortest days of the year, and the equinoxes are the midpoint in between. Since the beginning of agrarian society, we have marked these times as times for planting and harvesting, feasting and rest. The Winter Solstice celebrates the return of the sun, as days begin growing longer, so festivals of light are common around the world. At the Spring Equinox, the ground begins to thaw, seeds begin to sprout, and we celebrate rebirth and renewal, a time full of color. The Summer Solstice celebrates the peak of fertility, with sexual and transformative rites. And the Autumnal Equinox is time for a great harvest feast and to celebrate the abundance of diverse expressions of Devi.

Celebration of the Birth of the Living Goddess

The birthday of your personal Living Goddess is a time for celebration and gratitude. You serve Her well all year, but on the anniversary of Her birth it is time to stop everything and just recognize the important role She plays in your life. Devotees should place the Goddess upon a throne, surrounded by opulence and beauty, and make offerings of things She loves. Write poetry and songs in Her honor and enjoy a feast of her favorite foods. Look to this day as your Hive's New Year.

Yoni Puja

Yoni puja is the worship of the yoni - the female sexual anatomy, as the symbol of the cosmic source of all. The yoni of a Woman at the peak fertile time of her cycle is preferred, although sculptures and yoni-shaped stones may be used in her place. Men occupying their "animal nature" and not ready to show respect and reverence should not be included. There are similarities to daily puja, with elemental offerings and gifts and mantras chanted. Liquids are poured over the yoni and collected in a vessel, and the resulting mixture is sipped by all participants. Participants may make wishes upon the yoni or ask for blessings, and then there is a period of contemplation of the yoni before the puja is done.

Menses

Menses are the time of rest for all Women. A Woman may mark her "red tent days" (the time of heaviest bleeding, usually at the start of her cycle) as times when she is not to be expected to take on any responsibilities. She should not even be expected to cook food for herself. This is a dedicated time for relaxation and extra pampering. She may get massages and enjoy free bleeding either in her own tub, outside in the garden (menstrual blood is great for fertilizing plants), or in a section of a warm bath house dedicated to this purpose. She may lay naked and be washed with hot flowing waters as she unlocks her pelvic muscles and releases all tension.

Rites of Passage

Isolation and Embrace

Every Hive should have a quiet room equipped with a shower, toilet, comfortable mattress, and a chair, with plain undecorated white walls. Every new initiate to the Hive must spend between 3 and 9 days alone, with no screens, no books, no entertainment, and no human interaction beyond the silent delivery of plain but healthy meals like quinoa, oats, soups, and smoothies.

We all must understand what kind of madness we suffer. This isolation period allows one to get in touch with one's own mind, untangle one's anxieties and neurosis, and understand our levels of patience and coping skills. It's also a detox from the noise of the world, a way to clear one's head.

Slowly books, music, and writing implements will be reintroduced to the initiate. Plant medicines may be administered, such as Bobinsana to help remove melancholy from the brain. They will then be brought out by the Queen and greeted by a small group of 3-5 members who have been through the same or similar process. The initiate will have an opportunity to process all the thoughts and feelings that moved through them during isolation and talk about ways to soothe their demons. They may go on walks and engage in physical exercise, and they will be given warm embraces to welcome them into the fold. After spending some time with the small group, they will be introduced to the larger community with a celebratory meal and given their own room or living space. The initiate may be given a day to acclimate before taking over any jobs or responsibilities they've been given, or, if they wish, they may be trained right away and jump right into the rhythm of the Hive.

Naming Ceremony

Upon being accepted into a Hive, Women are supported in choosing their own name, and their surname can be changed to the first name of a Woman in their family or a woman they admire. They may also choose to change their entire name or, conversely, affirm their love for their given name. Men may maintain their given name or petition their Queen or a female partner to be granted a new name, which is considered a high honor. Names may be changed legally at the state or county courthouse, and all members are given step-by-step instructions on how to do so. When a name is chosen, it will be entered into an official register, and there should be a ceremony to reintroduce them to the Hive. Every Hive member will greet them with their new name and offer a small symbolic gift. Their name will be chanted by the group followed by applause and celebration.

Relationship Ceremonies

When two or more people enter into official relationship contracts they may gather close family, friends, and/or all members of their Hive to witness their promises to one another and hold them accountable. It can be as casual or formal as they like. They may exchange symbols of their bond such as bracelets, rings, collars, or piercings. Indefinite contracts can be celebrated with a tattoo. Meaningful bonding rituals and gestures can be designed or requested from the Queen/Goddess or friends. Likewise, all other types of relationships may be celebrated and honored, such as friendships, mentorships, housemates, or business partnerships, with pledges and symbols exchanged in the same manner. After the ceremony, celebrants can be given three days off from all responsibilities to enjoy each other's company.

Introduction of a New Living Goddess

Whenever a new Living Goddess is introduced, She will hold darshan with all devotees. One by one, devotees will approach to bow at Her feet (and kiss them if She allows it) and make offerings. A lamp will be lit and presented to Her and she will in turn hold it in front of each devotee for a moment to share in its light together. Her name will be chanted by the group 108 times, followed by the ringing of the bell or gong. Matras or songs may be chanted or sung, according to Her wishes. If she has special roles planned for certain devotees, she will give those out to them at the first darshan, or devotees may approach and offer her their specific skills.

Temple Consecration

Living Goddesses may be in charge of building a Devi Temple. This is an art to which She should apply her intuition and individual vision while holding in mind some important elements of classical temple designs, such as placing the entrance in the East, and having a womb chamber that cannot be viewed from the entrance, where a permanent altar to the Goddess will be placed and puja will be performed daily. Altars and images of other expressions of Devi may also be included. Care must be taken to think about the movements of rituals and how the space can accommodate them with natural ease. The temple also must provide the proper atmosphere for devotees to enter and contemplate their Goddess at any time. When the temple is complete the entire Hive should attend the consecration, wherein Darshan is held and the first puja is performed.

Mourning Rites

When we lose anyone or face the end of a relationship or era in life, we must have ways to experience that mourning fully. Mourning rituals are held for the devotee with those closest to them. They are brought to a warm space and gently touched, anointed with oils, massaged, and embraced by those who love them. Here they will allow their emotions to flow. They may weep, moan, scream, or rage, and all the participants will echo their expression of emotions like a perfect mirror. When they weep softly the room weeps softly. When they shout the room shouts. If they wish to bring their painful feelings to the outside from deep within, they may include flagellation, piercing, or cutting, which unlocks repressed emotion. The goal of the ritual is that the mourning reaches a peak where the mourner has the sensation of taking flight, and then they are slowly brought back down for a gentle and affectionate landing amongst their loved ones.

Cremation

Cremation releases the final energies of the body to the absolute stillness of Siva. It is important that each member of a Hive write down their wishes for the handling of their cremation after death. They should enter into meditation before creating the document and be as detailed as possible about their funeral wishes. Their body will be taken to the crematorium if a traditional funeral pyre cannot be arranged. Their ashes may be spread in places of their choosing or shared among their Hive, friends, and family inside art or jewelry. In some cases, a dasa may want to make a tea and ingest a bit of his Goddess's ashes as part of his mourning ritual. Ashes may be kept on the altar and placed on the foreheads of devotees at the funeral, or stored in a display that honors the Hive's members who pass.

The Left Hand Path

These practices are not for everyone, and they take a deep dive into the Dark Feminine, dancing with shadows and playing with our hidden thoughts and emotions. The Left Hand path purposefully breaks taboos and gives our most disturbing mysteries a proper outlet so they do not become neglected and invade our everyday lives. We welcome the shadow and give whatever it holds a place to play. I will only share vague descriptions as these potent rites should be esoteric knowledge passed directly through the network of Gynarchy. They are to be kept in every Goddess's individual Book of Rites as she learns and leads them.

Repentance Ritual

In this ritual, men are allowed the opportunity to repent for the harms done by all men who came before them. Masochistic men stand in for those who have hurt us, and face painful retribution. This is an outlet for women's rage and men's guilt to be alchemized and absolved.

Ego Annihilation

This ritual helps to get the ego out of the way and helps the practitioner gain a more universal perspective. The strongholds of reactive ego resistance are discovered and systematically destroyed. This rite can take the participant through deep feelings of humiliation and then bring them back, relieved to be rid of that which sets off unwanted emotional triggers. It is a new freedom.

Dream Rituals

The Living Goddesses are known to enter into the dreams of their devotees and these rituals can be intentional group dreams where the participants then come together to talk about the symbols and emotions that showed up. This may provide answers to questions, or help the Hive have a clearer understanding of Devi's Desires, or it may simply be a bonding ritual between Devi and devotees.

Breathwork

There are breathing techniques that bring on altered states of consciousness even more powerfully than psychedelic drugs. The journeys taken through the process are individual and can be surprising, often allowing the breather to go back in time and deal with past traumas or even to return to the experience of their own birth. These rites work well for therapeutic sessions.

Succubus Rites

Imagine if the voice of the Living Goddess could be installed into your own mind to observe and guide you. What if she could be perfectly mentally cloned and rule you from within? A long process of meditations and hypnosis, often lasting six months, makes this possible.

Blood Sacraments

Rituals of piercing, cutting, and flesh pulling are powerful ways to enter into altered states of consciousness and have erotic and ecstatic experiences of Devi. A male who offers up his blood opens his body and mind in new ways and has the experience of Feminine seeing. He is lost in the Beloved. This can also expand the subject's resilience through rituals of endurance and ordeal.

Harvest of Sexual Energy

There are points throughout the year during which individual sexually active Women reach a peak of sexual arousal and desire. This can last a few days or a month. At that time the Woman is said to be ripe, and her libido becomes so strong that she can concentrate on little else. This is the best time to harvest sexual energy from the Hive toward specific intents. It is the time for sex magic. Various tantric techniques will be brought into play. Using the Woman's most taboo or highly charged sexual fantasies as a script, members of the Hive bring her eroticism to a frenzied crescendo, sharing in her ecstasy. They then speak the collective hopes and plans they wish to bring to fruition in the format of chants or rhymes.

Abortion Sacrament

Unplanned pregnancies should be rare within Hives, given the focus on sex education and women's choice. But if a woman has to make the unfortunate decision to terminate a pregnancy for whatever reason, she may return the potential of new life to Devi in a holy sacrament that helps her process the resulting grief. This is a Women's only rite performed in a small group.

| 4 - 5 |

Symbols

The Beckoning Heart - Cathexis

This is the Gynarchy symbol, designed by Viola Voltairine. The beckoning heart draws you into the mysteries of the Divine Feminine. It is symbolic of Cathexis, the feeling of intense focus on the Beloved, which pulls you to the center where Devi sits. The outer triangle is the Goddess, the individuated expression of Devi as Historic or Living Deity. The inner triangle is Devi ringed with the three realms of the knower, knowing and known, which wrap around her. The center circle is the infinite potential of all.

The Hibiscus Flower

The red Hibiscus is known as The Goddess Kali's flower. It symbolizes devotion, passion, protection, and the vibrant energy she embodies. It is representative of Her protruding tongue and blood lust, which rescued the world from demons in Indian mythology. In Gynarchy, it is also the symbol of the Five Steps the devotee takes when stepping onto the path of devotion: surrender, submit, sacrifice, serve, survive.

The Eight-Pointed Star

The eight-pointed star has classically been the symbol of the Goddess Ishtar/Inanna/Venus and has many symbolic meanings throughout history. It symbolizes the Eight Pillars of Gynarchy: Consent, Bodily Autonomy, Collaboration, Abundance, Networks, The Hive, Conflict Resolution, and The Feminine as Divine.

The Serpent

The serpent has always been associated with knowledge, whether as the one who tempts Eve to eat the fruit of the tree of knowledge or as the Naga serpent deities of India who led humans to knowledge. In the earliest creation myth, he is the first thing the Goddess of All creates, after separating the sky from the ocean. After they make love, she gives birth to the egg of the universe. In Devi Doctrine he is the Desire to Know, which sets off the creation of all that exists, in answer to Devi's question "What am I?" He sits coiled within all self-conscious beings.

PART 5

SHADOW AND VIRUS

Shadow

Carl Jung thought of the shadow as all those unconscious things within us that don't align with our ideal aim
or our ego's ideal vision of itself. Our conscious personality
sees these parts of ourselves as negative and may respond
to them with fear or disgust. The bigger the ego the bigger
the shadow it casts. But those things don't always stay put
in the ego's blind spot. They come into view at unexpected
moments. Cultures have massive shadows as well.

As I wrote this book, I began to understand a pattern.
All the negatives I attribute to patriarchy - war, conquest,
competition, the use of force - are all sourced in the emotions
of fear and anxiety. They are all about claiming and then
protecting what's yours. It's a kind of hypervigilance, like
someone always afraid of being hurt. Every offense is a kind
of defense.

And there's a lot of talk these days about "protecting
values." Every act of suppressing and oppressing the rights of

others is backed by the language of panicked defensive action. "If we don't stop them, they will win." "They will destroy what we stand for." It's all anxiety and fear.

What is it they are defending against? It is their own shadow. It is the parts of our shared human culture that they are trying to keep hidden and exiled. And those parts could be broadly defined as the Feminine. In the book *Shadow Culture,* Eugene Taylor discusses a kind of shadow spirituality that filters into the mainstream. These beliefs and practices have always been considered fringe in American society, yet surface within mainstream consciousness. White Anglo-Saxon Christians do yoga and talk about astrology. They comment casually about who they must have been in a past life. But these people are part of the Christian majority, and those beliefs are not part of the patriarchal Abrahamic faith.

Some surveys indicate that 70% of Gen Z (adults aged 18-24) in Western countries engage in some form of the occult from tarot reading to energy work to spellcasting. Those who stand firmly in a more masculine empiricist mindset will mock these things as "woo woo," and express disgust at those who give them any credence. They try to diminish the obvious society-wide influence. But this is the play of the Dark Feminine. The Shadow Feminine. Rabbi Jonathan Cahn was correct to take notice of the return of the Goddess. Even if you exile Her to the underworld like Persephone, She has a cyclical nature and will always return with the Spring. You can only oppress and ignore Her for so long before your anxiety starts to rise, and you find your shadow enveloping you. You can laugh Her off, or sound the alarms and man the defenses, but She is an innate part of all of human culture. She is, in fact, the very origin of it.

Virus

All social interaction is viral. Thoughts and ideas spread from one person, or one group, to the next. If we all spread a believable rumor to seven of our closest friends, that rumor would be heard by hundreds within days. Social media amplifies this effect. We are interconnected beings. Not just information and gossip, but moods and behaviors are also contagious.

In the book *Connected*, Dr. Nicholas A. Christakis and Dr. James H. Fowler identify cases of a phenomenon called MPI, mass psychogenic illness, otherwise known as mass social contagion. These cases range from sharing symptoms of an illness to unstoppable bouts of dancing or laughter, all of which share the same basic psychological process, and all of which involve emotions of fear and anxiety. These emotional stampedes are like the stampeding of buffalo. When one animal bolts, it triggers a cascade of fear that gets the whole herd moving.

Some viruses can be very damaging to social relationships, destroying connections and creating massive breaks and divisions. And, like emotional stampedes, they are the social viruses that infect us through the mechanisms of anxiety and fear. Our social immune system is compromised by these two emotions more than any other, making us susceptible to disease and distress in the social fabric.

If someone has an agenda to push, they need only inject

that agenda with the highly contagious emotional microbes of fear and anxiety, and it will spread faster than the common cold. And that's just what a group called the CNP, the Council for National Policy knows all too well.

Journalist Anne Belson compiled her investigation of the organization, and all its offshoots and connections, in the appropriately titled book *Shadow Network.* They began in 1981 as a group of archconservatives who realized the tides were turning, and by 2031, if things kept going as they were, their voter base would have died off and been replaced by much more liberal-leaning voters. They dreamed of returning to 19th-century religious patriarchy, which limited civil rights for all but white Protestant male property owners and provided no safety nets for the poor. Women, minorities, and gays, who were quickly beginning to gain political influence, were standing in their way.

They had a strategy. As local radio stations and newspapers in middle America began to collapse in the 2000s because of financial problems, the CNP swept in to fill the vacuum. It didn't help that the political power players had little respect for the people in what they arrogantly referred to as "flyover country" between coasts. It created the perfect marriage of disenfranchised voters and a unified media voice with carefully curated messages filled to the brim with fear and anxiety. And they proposed a remedy for that anxiety: the return to "traditional values." For them that meant conservative Evangelical values, homophobia, male dominance, and not taxing the rich. They took up the defensive rallying cry that their audience was "under attack" by liberals. They put that message on repeat not only on local radio stations and newspapers, but later on television and online as well. Belson begins the book with a cast of characters and groups who came together to orchestrate and fund the message, from fundamentalist preachers to the CEO of Blackwater, from the American Family Association to Breitbart, all with connections through the CNP.

The enemy targets of this campaign of anxiety were minorities, immigrants, unions, gays, and of course, feminist women. Together, they were all leading to America's downfall. The warring "us vs. them" psychology was in full force. "Be afraid. Protect what's yours." And one of the predictable results was a wave of misogyny that swept America.

Male anxiety - a deadly combination of entitlement and fear of irrelevance and humiliation - is one of the most potent kinds of anxiety on the planet. It has killed more men through war, colonialism, and just plain reckless behavior than all of the bacteria, viruses, and parasites combined. And it kills women right along with them.

When activated it leads to things like Gamergate, where, in the summer of 2014, thousands of men sent death threats to game developer Zoe Quinn, instigated by her former boyfriend. Later even more were sent to female gaming journalist Anita Sarkeesian. A campaign of ceaseless harassment began because she pointed out that women were treated badly within their community. Men doxed her, sharing her address and personal information and making it impossible to feel safe in her home. These male gamers felt women were invading "their" space and would run them out with threats of rape and violence. It was another case of "claim what's yours and protect it!" The fear of being humiliated by women in the highly competitive space of video games was overwhelming.

The internet has provided gathering places for all manner of angry young men, who have been told they are entitled to the world by virtue of being male but can't seem to get a girlfriend. "Incel" (involuntary celibate) culture is outwardly hateful toward women. And members will often infer, or outright state, that women should be required to have sex with men if they are "nice."

I'm reminded of my own father. When I was in my 20's my parents divorced, and my dad decided to go online after angrily resisting it for years. It was where my mom found her new boyfriend, after all, so it had negative associations for him. Not long after he jumped into the web, he began referring to himself as "MGTOW," part of a subculture of heterosexual "men going their own way." They were tired of trying to make relationships work, so they were going to focus on themselves and find happiness as single men. They would enjoy their lives, drama free.

It sounded like a positive self-help movement. But when I went into their online forums and websites it consisted of 90% misogynistic jokes and criticisms of women, some confessing that they wish they could kill us. There was very little about being better men or enjoying life. It was a non-stop hate-filled bitchfest about the opposite sex, mixed in with lascivious ramblings about very young girls. For men who had decided to give up women, they sure did think about us nonstop.

Now, I'd known my dad my whole life, so I knew he had a very dark, pedophilic, and even a bit antisocial side, and he tended to think of himself as smarter than everyone in the room. I also realized later that he had all of the textbook symptoms of autism spectrum disorder: Lack of eye contact, no understanding of social cues, no interest in personal hygiene, and intense special interests that he would talk about ad nauseam, regardless of whether or not the listener was interested. As a kid, he would take apart every mechanical and electronic item he could get his hands on and then put it back together again. And, of course, he had been badly bullied in school. So his ability to understand social dynamics was understandably hampered by his "neurospicy" brain.

However, throughout my life, I had witnessed him in his happy moments. In his smiling, contented, enthusiastic moments where he was really in his element. And most of those times were when he was working hard to help my mom or me with some project. He fixed up my first car for me from junk, he helped my mom set up a studio and editing suite so she could make wedding videos and local TV commercials, and he helped me with my video projects when I was in art school. He briefly had a girlfriend and was constantly doing repairs for her and helping her with the technical aspects of her business. And when he was being useful like that, he was absolutely full of joy.

But while he was under the influence of MGTOW, if I had said, "You know you seem at your best when you are serving the women in your life," he would have gotten red in the face with rage and he would have ranted about how all women are just users. All they want him for is what he can do for them! He had already said such things about his girlfriend after they broke up.

And that's because, in this culture of male dominance and male anxiety, he was supposed to be the man - the one in charge, the one being catered to. The language of "serving" women would bring into question his whole superior male identity, even though serving was where he was at his best and most personally fulfilled. Being useful was, in fact, his happy place.

But the cognitive dissonance around the word "serving" would be much too much. Instead of doing what he actually liked doing, he'd twisted it into not getting enough transactional benefit. The rationale became, "I did this for you, and, being a man, I am therefore contractually owed sex and affection as payment." That's like turning every heterosexual romantic relationship into sex work. In the minds of men who follow this logic, every woman is a prostitute, and every man is a john. And if they aren't, then the man is somehow automatically humiliated. The fear of humiliation always drives the narrative. My dad was trying to hang onto male dominance so hard that he turned himself into nothing more than a consumer, rather than a lover, of women. All because of an anxiety generated by other men about his shadow - the tender and giving part of himself that, if seen, would be met with shame and disgust.

This is where the Gynarchy movement can rescue a great number of men.

I loved a season of the show *American Horror Story* called *Cult.* In one of the punchiest lines in the season finale, Sarah Paulson's character looks at her adversary, a sociopath misogynist cult leader bent on cultivating fear to gain political power, and she retorts, "You were wrong. There is something more dangerous in this world than a humiliated man. It's a nasty woman."

And I like this line, not in the competitive villain-gets-slain way in which it occurs in the show, however, but in a very different sense. The Shadow Feminine - sexy, mysterious, dark - is more dangerous to the status quo than the men sick with the anxiety of humiliation. The "nasty woman" - Inanna, Ishtar, Lilith, Kali, The Witch, The Dakini, The Dominatrix - has the power to change the direction of society. And in doing so, to relieve men of their constant worry and tension over their place and purpose in it.

If men can be proud of what naturally makes them genuinely happy - which, in many cases, is being used well by the women they love, pouring their love into us, and seeing the smiles upon our faces when we're pleased with their competence - instead of seeing it as a failure to live up to the male dominant nonsense and feeling embarrassed about it, then life will be better for everyone.

There are quite a number of men who have discovered this. I refer to them as "evolved men," because they've played in the shadows and are now ready and equipped for the next phase of social evolution.

Non-Violent Revolution

In her 2014 Ted Talk, political scientist Erica Chenoweth discussed her surprising discovery about Revolutions. Contrary to what she had assumed, violent uprisings and insurgencies are far less successful and do not create as much long-lasting change as non-violent movements. At first, she insisted that non-violent resistance could not work to upend dictators or start new countries. And someone said to her, "If you're right, then prove it." She ended up proving herself wrong. Her data covered the entire world over the previous 100 years and included instances that involved 1000 or more participants. Non-violent campaigns were twice as likely to succeed, even in brutal authoritarian conditions. And that trend is increasing over time.

So it stands to reason, if we want Gynarchy to have a broad cultural influence and even political power, it won't happen as a result of a sudden forceful revolt against patriarchy. And we cannot become isolationists, cut off from the broader cultures within which we are nested. We will have to take some tips from movements that succeed at influencing because people want to be influenced. Because the people in their lives, whom they care about, pass on that influence. It must be a social evolution.

In the novel *The Quickening*, when women begin taking over, they do so by going offline. They write letters and pass around newsletters and zines, and the novelty of it makes it seem precious. The main spokeswoman is a pop star who rejects the media and leaves the limelight, posting a simple website with the address to her P.O. Box and a link to the manifesto, *The Quickening*. As the world spirals into war and chaos, the movement is able to spread from one woman to another, the old-fashioned way.

There is something to that notion, though becoming Luddites is a mistake. Large social media platforms that devolve into virtual shouting matches like Twitter/X and Facebook/Meta are good places to use as billboards or teases, as they reach lots of eyes. But the potential for sophisticated conversations and real connection is rather limited (not impossible, just more difficult). I recall the early days of social media, and of LiveJournal, when we all wrote very long and personal posts and came to know one another as friends. In 2000, I created a website with bulletin boards and amassed a community of 5000 people. A few dozen of us would chat with each other multiple times per day.

The technology isn't the problem. It's the format. We now have more intimate possibilities like small Discord servers and Telegram groups where we can have lasting in-depth conversations without harassment from trolls. We can create Mistress groups that get together on Zoom calls and work through personal problems and give each other live, uplifting support. We can begin Hives online and then move them into physical locations after careful planning. We won't hand out our entire ideology in the mass market web spaces as much as drop hints about it, keeping it mysterious.

Let people buy books, pick up zines in random places, and find their way into our privately controlled spaces if they want to know the full story. Those who want a discussion are welcome, and those who want a fight can be sent on their way and blocked. There's no point in becoming entangled in gotchas and circular debates over strawmen. No ideology is bulletproof, nor does it need to be, unless it's being attacked. And unless you're being harmed by the ideology somehow, attacking it is pointless. No one is forcing anyone to become a Gynarchist. Conflict Resolution is one of our pillars. If we can't win an ally through empathy or playfulness, chances are the person's intentions were never sincere to begin with.

We must make it a point to have real conversations with real people, one-on-one. Don't try to get onto adversarial podcasts and talk shows where men speak over us, and our soundbites can be remixed and taken out of context. We should build our small communities, but also surprise others when we show up in large groups to events and talks. Create classes and courses for women and men. Make personal connections with people as we learn together. The more well-connected each of us is, the fewer degrees of separation between us and those we want to know.

Men can take an active role by offering random acts of service and kindness to women and giving them gifts of books like this one. Expect nothing in return, and if they engage you in conversation maybe you'll get around to talking about Gynarchy as a philosophy. Show women you are happy to support them and care about their desires. Become visible as a man who serves women. Get through that fear of humiliation. It serves no one.

And all Gynarchists can be giving, and charitable, and if someone says thank you, say, "No problem. I'm a Gynarchist and abundance is one of our main pillars." Don't ask them to get involved, just leave it at that and let them inquire if they are curious. Remember that the Feminine is attractive, magnetic. We attract but we don't proselytize. And if someone is hostile to our movement, we can let them be without engaging in heated debate. It is normal for differing ideologies to co-exist. Any conversion happens through connection and not by crusade.

"There is increasing evidence that religion and the inclination to form social networks are both part of our biological heritage and that the two may be related. Religion is one means of integrating people into a collective. A belief in God can have relevance to social networks in a very direct way: God can actually be seen as part of the social network. This involves not just the personification of a deity but the addition of a deity into the social fabric."

"One way to make social networks stable is to arrange them so that everyone is connected to a node that can never be removed. There would then be a short path from each person to every other person through this particular node. But even the most popular person in a society could not fill this role since, realistically, a single individual cannot be connected to absolutely everyone. And even if someone could be so connected, the effect on the network would not be permanent because humans are mortal." (Christakis and Fowler)

Devi is the irremovable immortal node connecting each Gynarchist directly to one another. And if you are already involved with women's groups, you probably already know women interested in the Divine Feminine. Whether she is a monotheist who believes in God as Mother, or a polytheist who works with multiple Goddesses, she is already an honorary Gynarchist, even if she has never heard the word.

Network is not one of the Eight Pillars of Gynarchy just

because our hives are interconnected. We should look for points of connection with other groups as well. Pagans, Unitarian churches, anarchists, mutual aid groups, intentional community organizations, ecological activists, and others can be our allies.

We can network through the arts, too. Music, theater, film, and dance are all collective pursuits. Look to the Pillar of Collaboration and find ways to combine talents. Project a Gynarchic sensibility via the Feminine's native language of creativity.

It may be, due to overexposure and overuse, the potent fear and anxiety mechanism of social contagion is running its course. As any health-threatening virus moves through the human population, our immune systems eventually learn how to protect against it, or we discover vaccines and can inoculate against it. Perhaps Gynarchists can become the inoculant to fear and open the hearts and eyes of those we meet. Regardless, it is inevitable that when it comes to the societies we live in, even if they don't play with Her in a conscious way as we do, they will always meet Devi in the shadows.

In the Spirit of networking and collaboration, please feel free to make use of my contact info:

Viola Strepsata Voltairine
viola.voltairine@gmail.com
The Cathexis Company, Ltd.
6525 Gunpark Dr, Suite 370, Box 106
Boulder, Colorado 80301

Surrender, Submit, Sacrifice, Serve, Survive
To Her, For Her, Through Her

NOTES

Step into my library and indulge in a deeper dive into any topic I've discussed.

Satisfy your Desire to Know.

Foreword and Acknowledgements

1. Tolokonnikova, Nadya. *Read & Riot: A Pussy Riot Guide to Activism*. HarperOne. 9 Oct 2018.
2. Ekata, Nithya. "*From the Etruscan Goddess Vatika to the Vatican*". Art-A-Tsolum. 9 Feb 2022. <https://tinyurl.com/yrm5j8yr> Accessed Aug 2023.
3. Emba, Christine. "*Men are lost. Here's a map out of the wilderness*". Washington Post. 10 Jul 2023. <https://tinyurl.com/45cx6rcs> Accessed Aug 2023.
4. Sussman, Anna Louie. "*A World Without Men: The women of South Korea's 4B movement aren't fighting the patriarchy - they're leaving it behind entirely*". The Cut, March 8, 2023. <https://tinyurl.com/5svu9ht9> Accessed Aug 2023.
5. Matos, Greg. "*What's Behind the Rise of Lonely, Single Men: Men need to address their deficits to meet healthier relationship expectations*". Psychology Today, 9 August 2022. <https://tinyurl.com/yz4tktz9> Accessed Aug 2023.

Part 1: The Reasons

1. Marina. *Man's World*. Ancient Dreams in a Modern Land. Atlantic Records. 2021.

1-1 The Stories We Tell

1. Voltairine, Viola. *150 Years of Gynarchy*. Artvamp, March 1, 2021.
2. ChatGPT. *"The Potential Advantages of Matriarchy: A Paradigm Shift Towards Equality and Balance"*. 21 Jul 2023. Accessed Jul 2023.
3. Pinker, Steven. *The Better Angels of Our Nature: Why Violence Has Declined*. Viking. 4 Oct 2011.
4. Tesla, Nicola. Interview conducted by Kennedy, John B. Colliers Magazine. 30 Jan 1926. <https://tinyurl.com/35v6dvjf> Accessed Jul 2023.
5. Alderman, Naomi. *The Power*. Little, Brown and Company. 27 Oct 2016.
6. Caro, Robert. *The Power Broker*. Alfred A. Knopf. 12 Jul 1974.
7. Riley, Talulah. *The Quickening*. Hodder & Stoughton. 23 Jun 2022.
8. Sawers, Mark, director. *No Men Beyond This Point*. Samuel Goldwyn Films, 2015. 1h 21m. Trailer: <youtu.be/lFgditcE7gU> Accessed Jul 2023.

1-2 Gynarchy Defined

1. Voltairine, Viola. *150 Years of Gynarchy*. Artvamp, 1 Mar 2021.
2. Humm, Maggie. *The Dictionary of Feminist Theory (Second Edition)*. Edinburgh University Press. 16 Oct 2003.
3. Justice, Jason. *Defining Anarchism*. TheAnarchistLibrary.org. 1 Jan 2005. <https://tinyurl.com/2p89275j> Accessed Aug 2023.

1-3 The Argument Against Egalitarian Society

1. Robbins, Matthew, director. *Legend of Billie Jean*. Delphi III Productions. 1985. 1h 36m. Trailer: <youtu.be/FTyHPlRVTPI>. Accessed Jul 2023.
2. U.S. Federal Bureau of Investigation, 2012. Crime in the U.S. Table 42 Arrests. FBI.gov. <https://tinyurl.com/ycy2phub> Accessed Jul 2023.

3. Bader Ginsburg, Ruth. Commencement speech Georgetown University. 9 Feb 2015.

4. *"Study finds PTSD effects may linger in body chemistry of next generation."* uploaded by PBS NewsHour. 30 Aug 2015. <youtu.be/zV9sya4F5KQ> Accessed Jul 2023.

5. Bale, Tracy L. *"Lifetime stress experience: transgenerational epigenetics and germ cell programming".* Dialogues in Clinical Neuroscience. 16 Sep 2014. <https://tinyurl.com/59nnj825> Accessed Jul 2023.

6. Quinn - Inlak'ech ND, Diana, *Healing Our Ancestors: The Importance of Ancestral Relationships.* Crazy Wisdom Publications. 1 May 2019.

7. Sheldrake, Rupert. *Morphic Resonance: The Nature of Formative Causation.* Park Street Press. 9 Sep 2009.

1-4 Fear of a Female-Led World

1. Gaines, Myron. *Why Do Women Deserve Less?* Fish and Fit Books. 14 Feb 2023.

2. Stern, Scott W. *"America's Forgotten Mass Imprisonment of Women Believed to Be Sexually Immoral".* A+E Network's History Channel. 29 Mar 2019. <https://tinyurl.com/mth8tmtd> Accessed Jul 2023.

3. Council of Europe Parliamentary Assembly. Resolution 1681 (2009). Assembly debate 26 Jun 2009 (26th Sitting). <https://tinyurl.com/yc5he7mc> Accessed Jul 2023.

4. Maines, Rachel P. *The Technology of Orgasm: "Hysteria", the Vibrator, and Women's Sexual Satisfaction.* The Johns Hopkins University Press. 18 Dec 1998.

5. Hawthorne, Nathaniel. *The Scarlet Letter.* Ticknor, Reed and Fields. 1850.

6. Freud, Sigmund. *Three Essays on the Theory of Sexuality.* Sigmund Freud. 1905.

Part 2: The Foundations

1. Kesha. *Rich, White, Straight Men.* RCA Records. 8 Jun 2019. <youtu.be/M32Jnxa7dqE> Accessed Jul 2023.

2-1 The Eight Pillars of Gynarchy

1. Kant, Immanuel. *The Metaphysics of Morals (1797) (Second Edition)*. Mary J. Gregor, trans. Cambridge University Press. 31 May 1996.

2. Wahl, Daniel Christian. "*The Importance of Moving from 'Me' to 'We'*." UPLIFT Foundation. 2021. <https://tinyurl.com/2p9ds4p3> Accessed Jul 2023.

3. Shindler, David. "*Are Women More Collaborative and Men More Competitive?*" LinkedIn. 2 Oct 2018. <https://tinyurl.com/4axy29zx> Accessed Jul 2023.

4. Gaskell, Adi. "*Women Still Less Likely To Be Perceived As Leaders.*" Horizons Tracker. 14 Sep 2018. <https://tinyurl.com/54ykuc99> Accessed Jul 2023.

5. Fuller, R. Buckminster and Barlow, Elizabeth. "*The New York Magazine Environmental Teach-In*". New York Magazine. 30 Mar 1970.

6. Urbaniak, Kasia. *Unbound: A Woman's Guide to Power*. Tarcher Perigee. 8 Mar 2022.

7. Heide, Chantal. *Fix That Shit: A Couples Guide To Getting Past The Sticky Stuff*. CreateSpace. 7 Dec 2016.

8. Heide, Chantal. "*How do you NOT fight?*" YouTube. 26 Jan 2023. <youtu.be/e0ApYxiwXeo> Accessed Jul 2023.

9. Stone, Merlin. *When God Was a Woman*. Harcourt, Inc. 4 May 1978.

2-2 The Gender Binary

1. Justin Folk, director. *What is a Woman?* performance by Matt Walsh. The Daily Wire. 1 Jun 2023. Accessed Jul 2023.

2-3 The Nature of the Feminine

1. Vandermeer, Jeffery. *Annihilation*. Farrar, Straus and Giroux. 4 Feb 2014.

2. Garland, Alex, director. *Annihilation*. 2018. Netflix,Paramount Pictures. 1h 55m.

3. Graves, Robert. *The Greek Myths*. Penguin Books. 1 Jan 1955.

4. Monaghan, Patricia. *The New Book of Goddesses & Heroines (Third edition)*. Llewellyn Publications. 1 Jan 1997.

5. *"Oldest Genesis Myth in the World is SHOCKING"*. YouTube. uploaded by Gnostic Informant. 22 May 2023. <youtu.be/Dh7hgok-UiH4> Accessed Aug 2023.

2-4 Our Roles

1. Urbaniak, Kasia. 15 Oct 2019. *"One simple trick to reclaim your power."* TED Conferences. <youtu.be/9W1_vUiMC6E> Accessed Jul 2023

Part 3: Gynarchy-Aligned Education

3-1 History

1. Natarajan, Harini. *What Is Matriarchy? A Brief History Of Matriarchal Societies*. StyleCraze. 13 Jul 2023. <https://tinyurl.com/3v78mtmk> Accessed Jul 2023.

2. Zinsser, Judith. *Emilie Du Chatelet: Daring Genius of the Enlightenment*. Penguin Books. 27 Nov 2007.

3. Zielinski, Sarah. *Hypatia, Ancient Alexandria's Great Female Scholar*. Smithsonian Magazine. 14 Mar 2010. <https://tinyurl.com/3awejp7e> Accessed Jul 2023.

4. Wheatley, Phillis. *Phillis Wheatley, Complete Writings*. Penguin Classics. 1 Feb 2001.

5. Harper, Francis EW. *The Complete Frances Harper*. Mint Editions. 8 Jun 2021.

6. Diepenbrock, George. *"Art, religious artifacts support idea of Minoan matriarchy on ancient Crete, researcher says"*. University of Kansas. 13 Jun 2017. <https://tinyurl.com/3yf3k3vx> Accessed Aug 2023.

7. Rosenthal, Michael, narrator. *"Queen Arawelo"*. RetroPod. The Washington Post. 10 Apr 2019. <https://tinyurl.com/49j22nhy> Accessed Aug 2023.

8. Bindel, Julie. *"The village where men are banned"*. The Guardian. 16 Aug 2015. <https://tinyurl.com/3yjnbmev> Accessed Aug 2023.

9. Hart, Carol. *"For the Next 7 Generations: The Grandmothers Speak"* YouTube. 27 Jun 2007. <youtu.be/GKGXpK8LXR4> Accessed Aug 2023.

10. Miles, Rosalind. *Who Cooked the Last Supper: The Women's History of the World. Crown;* Three Rivers Press ed. edition, 10 April 2001.

11. Patel, Raj and Moore, Jason W. *A History of the World in Seven Cheap Things.* University of California Press. 17 Oct 2017.

3-2 Biology

1. Weber, Andreas. *Enlivenment: Towards a fundamental shift in the concepts of nature, culture and politics.* Heinrich-Böll-Stiftung. 2013.

2. Konner, Melvin. *Women After All: Sex, Evolution, and the End of Male Supremacy.* W. W. Norton & Company. 14 Mar 2016.

3. Griffin, Darren and Ellis, Peter. *"The Y chromosome is disappearing - so what will happen to men?"* University of Kent. 13 Feb 2018. <https://tinyurl.com/mr2kvazk> Accessed Jul 2023.

4. Robert, Martin D. *"The Macho Sperm Myth: The idea that millions of sperm are on an Olympian race to reach the egg is yet another male fantasy of human reproduction".* Aeon. 32 August 2018. <https://tinyurl.com/3xamdvru> Accessed Aug 2023.

5. University of Manchester staff. *"Human eggs prefer some men's sperm over others, research shows".* The University of Manchester. 10 Jun 2020. <https://tinyurl.com/5n6fem5m> Accessed Aug 2023.

6. Wahl, Daniel Christian. *"Life's economy is primarily based on collaborative rather than competitive advantage".* Medium. 1 Feb 2017. <https://tinyurl.com/4dyhmjuj> Accessed Jul 2023.

3-3 Economics

1. Patel, Raj and Moore, Jason W. *A History of the World in Seven Cheap Things.* University of California Press. 17 Oct 2017.

2. Wahl, Daniel Christian. *"Life's economy is primarily based on collaborative rather than competitive advantage."* Medium. 1 Feb 2017. <https://tinyurl.com/4dyhmjuj> Accessed Jul 2023.

3. Armbrust, Jennifer. *Proposals for the Feminine Economy.* In-

dependently Published. 7 Dec 2018. <https://sister.is/> Accessed Jul 2023.

4. Zurer, Rachel. *"Could a More Feminine Economy Save The World?"* SO-CAP Digital, 26 January 2018. <https://tinyurl.com/3mfk7349> Accessed Aug 2023.

5. Peng, Christina. *"Peng '26: Why most gift economies fail."* The Brown Daily Herald. 16 Sep 2022. <https://tinyurl.com/2p8jkvzh>. Accessed Aug 2023.

6. Pendleton, Madeline. *I Survived Capitalism and All I Got Was This Lousy T-Shirt.* Doubleday. 16 Jan 2024.

3-4 Psychology

1. Kaiser, Tim and Del Giudice, Marco and Booth, Tom. *"Global sex differences in personality: Replication with an open online dataset".* Wiley Online Library. 15 Jul 2019. < https://tinyurl.com/2dsb73js> Accessed Jul 2023.

2. Baron-Cohen, Simon and S. Wheelwright. *"The empathy quotient: an investigation of adults with Asperger syndrome or high functioning autism, and normal sex differences."* Journal of Autism and Developmental Disorders. Apr 2004. <https://tinyurl.com/3jxcxrff> Accessed Jul 2023.

3. Furfaro, Hannah. *"The extreme male brain, explained".* Spectrum News. 1 May 2019. <https://tinyurl.com/5h5x4ua9> Accessed Jul 2023.

4. Williams Woolley, Anita. *"Evidence for a Collective Intelligence Factor in the Performance of Human Groups."* Science. 30 Sep 2010. < https://tinyurl.com/bdeks3bz> Accessed Jul 2023.

5. Eagly, Alice H and Johnson, Blair T. *"Gender and leadership style: A meta-analysis."* Univ. of Connecticut Center for Health, Intervention, and Prevention. 1 Jan 1990. <https://tinyurl.com/44by7b24> Accessed Jul 2023.

6. Christensen, Jen. *"All around the world, women are better empathizers than men, study finds."* CNN Health & Climate. 26 Dec 2022. <https://tinyurl.com/nhenjzvk> Accessed Jul 2023.

7. Amen, Daniel G. *Unleash the Power of the Female Brain: Supercharging Yours for Better Health, Energy, Mood, Focus, and Sex*. Harmony. 12 Feb 2013.

8. Fielding, Sarah. *"Despite Culturally Ingrained Stereotypes, Women Are Not More Emotional Than Men"*. VeryWell Mind. 9 Nov 2021. <https://tinyurl.com/2p97xe22> Accessed Jul 2023.

9. "Gender differences in suicide". Wikimedia Foundation. 9 Aug 2023. <https://tinyurl.com/8bmmep72> Accessed Aug 2023.

10. Aggarwal-Schifellite, Manisha. *"How spanking may affect brain development in children"*. The Harvard Gazette. 12 Apr 2021. <https://tinyurl.com/2bh737hn> Accessed Aug 2023.

11. Dewar, Gwen. *"Authoritarian parenting outcomes: What happens to the kids?"* Parenting Science. 2016. <https://tinyurl.com/mtbxtukr> Accessed Aug 2023.

12. Tarrant, Jeffery. *"The Therapeutic Potential of Altered States of Consciousness"*. Psychology Today. 20 May 2022. <https://tinyurl.com/4ws76nbp> Accessed Jul 2023.

13. Grof, Christina and Grof, Stanislav. *Spiritual Emergency: The Understanding and Treatment of Transpersonal Crises*. International Journal of Transpersonal Studies volume 36, issue 2. 1 Sep 2017. <https://tinyurl.com/yc3xa2tz> Accessed Aug 2023.

14. Jung, Carl. *Alchemical Studies, Collected Works of C.G. Jung*, Volume 13. Princeton University Press. 1967.

3-5 World Religions

1. Alderman, Naomi. *The Power*. Little, Brown and Company. 27 Oct 2016.

2. Cahn, Jonathan. *The Return of the Gods*. Charisma Media. 6 Sep 2022.

3. *"Gospel of Philip"*. Wesley W. Isenberg, trans. *Early Christian Writings*. <https://tinyurl.com/2s3epnnm> Accessed Jul 2023.

4. *"Gospel of Mary"*. Berlin Gnostic Codex (Papyrus Berolinensis 8502). <https://tinyurl.com/54j2zsap> Accessed Jul 2023.

5. King James Bible 1769/2019, 1 Corinthians 14. Christian Art Publishers. Accessed Jul 2023.

6. *"Cult of the Virgin Mary."* Intriguing History. 8 Mar 2016. <https://tinyurl.com/yc7wztfx> Accessed Jul 2023.

7. Bauer, Pat. *Druids: ancient Celtic culture.* Encyclopedia Britannica, 11 August 2023. <https://www.britannica.com/topic/Druid> Accessed Aug 2023.

8. Mother Meera. *Answers Part 1.* Meeramma Publications. 1 Jan 1991.

9. Berendt, Joachim. *The World Is Sound: Nada Brahma.* Destiny Books. 1 May 1991.

10. Dyczkowski, Mark SG. *The Doctrine of Vibration: An Analysis of the Doctrines and Practices Associated with Kashmir Shaivism.* SUNY Press. 1 Jan 1987.

11. Muller-Ortega, Paul E. *The Triadic Heart of Siva: Kaula Tantricism of Abhinavagupta in the Non-Dual Shaivism of Kashmir.* State University of New York Press. 23 Nov 1988.

12. Adiyogi. *"More Witches Are Needed On The Planet! | Women | Feminine | Goddess| Sadhguru |Adiyogi"*. YouTube. 6 Mar 2023. <youtu.be/C6xAklaVz1U> Accessed Aug 2023.

13. *"Kumari Goddess: The Last Living Goddess of Nepal"*. Nepal Sanctuary Treks. 14 Jul 2018. <https://tinyurl.com/2sxzas36> Accessed Aug 2023.

14. Kohn, Livia. *Daoism: A Contemporary Philosophical Investigation (Investigating Philosophy of Religion).* Routledge. 10 Oct 2019.

15. *"Akan Faith - Dharmic tenets in Ancient African Philosophy (Karma, Dharma, Reincarnation, Afterlife)"*. YouTube. uploaded by Journey of the seeker. 13 Nov 2020. <youtu.be/0xse_pC1pq0> Accessed Aug 2023.

3-6 Sociology

1. Sear, Rebecca. *"The male breadwinner nuclear family is not the 'traditional' human family, and promotion of this myth may have adverse health consequences"*. The Royal Society Publishing. 3 May 2021. <https://tinyurl.com/5n862n8t> Accessed Aug 2023.

2. de Cleyre, Voltairine. "*Sex Slavery-A Lecture*". Unity Congregation, Philadelphia. 1890.

3. de Cleyre, Voltairine and Presley, Sharon. *Exquisite Rebel: The Essays of Voltairine de Cleyre: Feminist, Anarchist, Genius: They Who Marry do Ill.* State University of New York Press. 10 Feb 2005. < https://tinyurl.com/2ubh6wy7> Accessed Jul 2023.

4. Somers, Jeff. "*Popular Wedding Traditions With Creepy Origins*". Grunge.com. 25 Jan 2023. <https://tinyurl.com/5wmudasw> Accessed Aug 2023.

5. Nowak, Claire. "*The Notably Unromantic Reason We Have Bridesmaids and Groomsmen at Weddings*". Reader's Digest. 30 Mar 2017. <https://tinyurl.com/46324mtc> Accessed Jul 2023.

6. Waugaman, Elisabeth P. "*Names and Identity: The Native American Naming Tradition*". Psychology Today. 8 Jul 2011. < https://tinyurl.com/mpmfar8p> Accessed Jul 2023.

7. Jodorowsky, Alejandro. *Psychomagic: The Transformative Power of Shamanic Psychotherapy.* Inner Traditions. 18 Jun 2010.

8. Tina, Cynthia. *Intentional Communities: Beginners Guide to Life in Cooperative Culture.* CommunityFinders.com. 16 Dec 2022. <https://tinyurl.com/4bkzvcn5> Accessed Aug 2023.

9. Tina, Cynthia. *Starter Guide to Intentional Communities.* published online at Foundation for Intentional Community.org. Oct 2021. <https://tinyurl.com/3rb9n3h7> Accessed Aug 2023.

10. BBC staff writer. "*Dunbar's number: Why we can only maintain 150 relationships*" BBC Future. 1 Oct 2019. <https://tinyurl.com/2s426mck> Accessed Aug 2023.

International Communities referenced:

Damanhur

- website: https://damanhur.org/
- YouTube Channel: youtu.be/pVIiIoyrHwM

The Bruderhof

○ website: https://www.bruderhof.com/
○ YouTube Channel: youtu.be/9ohC8cEcdOE

Findhorn

○ website: https://www.findhorn.org/
○ YouTube channel: youtu.be/DcfcgeJfoMY

3-7 Sex Education

1. McCall, Rosie. "*There's One Anatomy Fact That Almost No Man Seems To Know*". IFLScience.com. 7 Nov 2018. <https://tinyurl.com/kst9tvec> Accessed Aug 2023.
2. Millhone, Carly. "*Can Vaginas Get 'Loose?'*". Health.com. 5 Dec 2022. <https://tinyurl.com/mtnrnae8> Accessed Aug 2023.
3. Wuyts, Elise and Morrens, Manuel. "*The Biology of BDSM: A Systematic Review.*" The Journal of Sexual Medicine volume 29, issue 1. 20 May 2021. <https://tinyurl.com/yb6p78mr> Accessed Aug 2023.
4. Ambler, J. K., Lee, E. M., Klement, K., R., Loewald, T., Comber, E. M., Hanson, S. A., Cutler, B., Cutler, N. & Sagarin, B. J. (2017). *Consensual BDSM facilitates role-specific altered states of consciousness: A preliminary study.* Psychology of Consciousness: Theory, Research, and Practice, 4, 75-91. <https://tinyurl.com/45ux3nf4> Accessed Aug 2023.
5. Erickson, Jennifer and Sagarin, BJ. "*The prosocial sadist? A comparison of BDSM sadism and everyday sadism*". Northern Illinois Univ. Dept. of Psychology. 2021. 14 Aug 2020. <https://tinyurl.com/3d44jtxb> Accessed Aug 2023.
6. Sagarin, B., Cutler, B., Cutler, N., Lawler-Sagarin, K. and Matuszewich, L. "*Hormonal Changes and Couple Bonding in Consensual Sadomasochistic Activity*". National Library of Medicine. 19 Jun 2008. <https://tinyurl.com/536xhzfr> Accessed Aug 2023.
7. Sagarin, B., Lee, E. and Klement, K. "*Sadomasochism without*

Sex? Exploring the Parallels between BDSM and Extreme Rituals". Northern Illinois Univ. Dept. of Psychology. 1 Nov 2015. <https://tinyurl.com/mukhz9bw> Accessed Aug 2023.

3-8 Femdom as religion

1. Harrington, Lee. *Sacred Kink: The Eightfold Paths of BDSM and Beyond*. Mystic Productions Press. 1 Apr 2016.

2. Parsons, Jack. *Freedom Is A Two Edged Sword*. Falcon Press. 21 Sep 1989.

3. Anger, Kenneth, director. *Inauguration of the Pleasure Dome*. 1954. 38m.

4. Scrivner, Jordan. *Your boy loves, respects, and adores you: a noir thriller*. Justin Easteregg. 1 Jul 2023.

5. Kansa, Spencer. *Wormwood Star the Magickal Life of Marjorie Cameron*. Mandrake. 23 Apr 2020.

6. CameronParsonsFdn. "*Cinderella of the Wastelands*". YouTube. 2013. <youtu.be/NxMJONFDw_E> Accessed Aug 2023.

7. Grey, Peter. *The Red Goddess*. Scarlet Imprint. 21 Feb 2021.

8. Trans-States. "*Peter Grey - Becoming No-Man*" YouTube. 25 Feb 2017. <youtu.be/3Ec28pFmrE> Accessed Aug 2023.

9. Adler, Margot. *Drawing Down the Moon*. Penguin Books. 3 Oct 2006.

10. Federici, Sylvia. *Caliban and the Witch*. Autonomedia. 15 Sep 2004.

11. Golden Order. *The Gospel of Our Mother God*. published online at CreateSpace. 3 Sep 2008.

12. McDaid, Lee. "*Maids of the Silver Sisterhood*" Burtonport, Donegal Ireland - 1983". YouTube. 12 Jul 2018. <youtu.be/59KuV4tlk2I&t=73s> Accessed Aug 2023.

13. RoseTintedSpectrum. "*From Cult to Game Developer: The Story of St. Brides & The Silver Sisterhood Documentary*". YouTube. 4 Sep 2021. <youtu.be/D6ZAesOS_do> Accessed Aug 2023.

14. Rosemaidens. "*Aristasia Documentary Part 1: A Weekend at Miss Martindale's*". YouTube. 19 Dec 2006. <youtu.be/3hxVnKUrHU> Accessed Aug 2023.

15. Douglas, Nik and Slinger, Penny. *Sexual Secrets, The Alchemy of Ecstasy (First Edition)*. Destiny Books. 1 Jun 1979.

16. Service of Mankind Church. *Essemian Manifesto*. Self-Published. 1983. website: <https://darkside-goddess.org/> Accessed Jul 2023.

17. Von Werder, Rasa. *Woman Thou Art God: The New Religion for Women*. Lulu.com. 10 Nov 2020. website: <https://tinyurl.com/d8hcfte4> Accessed Jul 2023.

18. Voltairine, Viola. *150 Years of Gynarchy*. Artvamp, March 1, 2021.

Additional websites of note:

- ○ Madame Cleo DuBois <https://www.cleodubois.com/>
- ○ Fakir Musafar <https://fakir.org/>
- ○ Cybelians <https://www.cybelians.com/>
- ○ UGR <https://gynrep.com/>

Part 4: The Devi Doctrine

1. Sevdaliza. *Eden*. Shabrang. Twisted Elegance. 28 Aug 2020.

Part 5: Shadow and Virus

1. Taylor, Eugene. *Shadow Culture: Psychology and Spirituality in America*. Counterpoint. 1 Jun 1999.

2. Cahn, Jonathan. *The Return of the Gods*. Charisma Media. 6 Sep 2022.

3. Christakis, Nicholas A. and Fowler, James H. Connected: *The Surprising Power of Our Social Networks and How They Shape Our Lives - How Your Friends' Friends' Friends Affect Everything You Feel, Think, and Do*. Little, Brown and Spark. 28 Sep 2009.

4. Belson, Anne. *Shadow Network: Media, Money, and the Secret Hub of the Radical Right*. Bloomsbury Publishing. 29 Oct 2019.

5. Murphy, R. (writer) and Falchuk, B. (writer). 5 Sep 2017. *Cult.*

American Horror Story season 7. TV series season. Executive producers Ryan Murphy and Brad Falchuk. FX Network.

6. Chenoweth, Erica. 4 Nov 2013. "*The success of nonviolent civil resistance.*" TED Conferences. <youtu.be/YJSehRlU34w> Accessed Jul 2023.

7. Riley, Talulah. *The Quickening.* Hodder & Stoughton. 23 Jun 2022.

RESOURCES

Women and Power

For women who wish to break their "good girl" conditioning and radically transform their lives, I highly recommended taking courses at the Academy, run by Kasia Urbaniak. It has been a real source of wisdom and inspiration for me, and the women I have met have enriched my life in countless ways.

https://www.kasiaurbaniak.com/the-academy

Other influencers of note

The Real Voodoo Bae (Wisdom of the Feminine Divine):

https://linktr.ee/therealvoodoobae

Princella the Queen Maker, The High Powered Podcast (Community and Advice for Women):

https://www.princellathequeenmaker.com/

Prayers and meditations

My dasa, Brett, has compiled a book of prayers and meditations that are particularly beautiful and insightful.

https://20-569-328-346.com/2022/02/01/when-worlds-collide/

FIND YOUR HIVE

If the Pillars of Gynarchy inspire you and you wish to find the people with whom to build your Hive, or you want to find an existing Hive open to new members, fill out my quick survey, and I will begin acting as your connecting node in the Network. Tell me who and where you are, and what roles with which you identify to get the conversation started.

https://ThePillarsofGynarchy.com

ABOUT THE AUTHOR

After earning her MFA in Film, Viola Voltairine dove into the study of Indian philosophy and Sanskrit. She recently launched an international organization called The Company, where Women have their desires catered to by a carefully screened group of men. She founded Artvamp Films in 2000 and is currently working on a new film called *Finding Love*, based on the popular FemDom romance by Renee Lane, with a screenplay by Guinevere Turner (of *American Psycho* fame). She also teaches courses on female-led relationships, and mentors a small group of students in her *Succubus Tech* hypnosis and mind control program. Viola lives with her two beloved submissives, Drum and Robbi.

To learn more:
https://violavoltairine.com
https://gynarchy.io
Free 3-day FLR course for Men: https://obedient.love
All courses: https://cathexishouse.com
150 Years of Gynarchy: https://150YearsofGynarchy.com